# New Jersey

## THE THIRTEEN COLONIES

# New Jersey

CRAIG A. DOHERTY

KATHERINE M. DOHERTY

Facts On File, Inc.

## New Jersey

Facts On File, Inc.
132 West 31st Street
New York NY 10001

**Library of Congress Cataloging-in-Publication Data**
Doherty, Craig A.
    New Jersey / Craig A. Doherty and Katherine M. Doherty.
        p. cm. — (Thirteen colonies)
    Includes bibliographical references and index.
    ISBN 0-8160-5408-8
    Contents: First contacts—First settlements in New Jersey—The English in New Jersey—Life in Colonial New Jersey—Road to Revolution—The war for independence begins—The tide turns in the war for independence—The State of New Jersey—Building a nation.
    1. New Jersey—History—Colonial period, ca. 1600–1775—Juvenile literature. 2. New Jersey—History—1775–1865—Juvenile literature. [1. New Jersey—History—Colonial period, ca. 1600–1775. 2. New Jersey—History—1775–1865.] I. Doherty, Katherine M. II. Title.

    F137.D64 2005
    974.9—dc22                  2003027477

Text design by Erika K. Arroyo
Cover design by Semadar Megged
Maps and graph by Dale Williams

Printed in the United States of America

VB Hermitage 10 9 8 7 6 5 4 3 2 1

This book is printed on acid-free paper.

This book is dedicated to
the many students of all ages
we have worked with and taught over the years.

# Contents

# Note on Photos

Many of the illustrations and photographs used in this book are old, historical images. The quality of the prints is not always up to current standards, as in some cases the originals are from old or poor-quality negatives or are damaged. The content of the illustrations, however, made their inclusion important despite problems in reproduction.

# Introduction

In the 11th century, Vikings from Scandinavia sailed to North America. They explored the Atlantic coast and set up a few small settlements. In Newfoundland and Nova Scotia, Canada, archaeologists have found traces of these settlements. No one knows for sure why they did not establish permanent colonies. It may have been that it was too far away from their homeland. At about the same time, many Scandinavians were involved with raiding and establishing settlements along the coasts of what are now Great Britain and France. This may have offered greater rewards than traveling all the way to North America.

When the western part of the Roman Empire fell in 476, Europe lapsed into a period of almost 1,000 years of war, plague, and hardship. This period of European history is often referred to as the Dark Ages or Middle Ages. Communication between the different parts of Europe was almost nonexistent. If other Europeans knew about the Vikings' explorations westward, they left no record of it. Between the time of Viking exploration and Christopher Columbus's 1492 journey, Europe underwent many changes.

By the 15th century, Europe had experienced many advances. Trade within the area and with the Far East had created prosperity for the governments and many wealthy people. The Catholic Church had become a rich and powerful institution. Although wars would be fought and governments would come and go, the countries of Western Europe had become fairly strong. During this time, Europe rediscovered many of the arts and sciences that had

Vikings explored the Atlantic coast of North America in ships similar to this one. *(National Archives of Canada)*

existed before the fall of Rome. They also learned much from their trade with the Near and Far East. Historians refer to this time as the Renaissance, which means "rebirth."

At this time, some members of the Catholic Church did not like the direction the church was going. People such as Martin Luther and John Calvin spoke out against the church. They soon gained a number of followers who decided that they would protest and form their own churches. The members of these new churches were called Protestants. The movement to establish these new churches is called the Protestant Reformation. It would have a big impact on America as many Protestant groups would leave Europe so they could worship the way they wanted to.

In addition to religious dissent, problems arose with the overland trade routes to the Far East. The Ottoman Turks took control of the lands in the Middle East and disrupted trade. It was at this time that European explorers began trying to find a water route to the Far East. The explorers first sailed around Africa. Then an Italian named Christopher Columbus convinced the king and queen of Spain that it would be shorter to sail west to Asia rather than go around Africa. Most sailors and educated people at the time knew the world was round. However, Columbus made two errors in his calculations. First, he did not realize just how big the Earth is, and second, he did not know that the continents of North and South America blocked a westward route to Asia.

When Columbus made landfall in 1492, he believed that he was in the Indies, as the Far East was called at the time. For a period of time after Columbus, the Spanish controlled the seas and the exploration of what was called the New World. England tried to compete with the Spanish on the high seas, but their ships were no match for the floating fortresses of the Spanish Armada. These heavy ships, known as galleons, ruled the Atlantic.

In 1588, that all changed. A fleet of English ships fought a series of battles in which their smaller but faster and more maneuverable ships finally defeated the Spanish Armada. This opened up the New World to anyone willing to cross the ocean. Portugal, Holland, France, and England all funded voyages of exploration to the New World. In North America, the French explored the far north. The Spanish had already established colonies in what are now Florida, most of the Caribbean, and much of Central and South America. The

Depicted in this painting, Christopher Columbus completed three additional voyages to the Americas after his initial trip in search of a westward route to Asia in 1492. *(Library of Congress, Prints and Photographs Division [LC-USZ62-103980])*

Dutch bought Manhattan and would establish what would become New York, as well as various islands in the Caribbean and lands in South America. The English claimed most of the east coast of North America and set about creating colonies in a variety of ways.

Companies were formed in England and given royal charters to set up colonies. Some of the companies sent out military and trade expeditions to find gold and other riches. They employed men such as John Smith, Bartholomew Gosnold, and others to explore the lands they had been granted. Other companies found groups of Protestants who wanted to leave England and worked out deals that let them establish colonies. No matter what circumstances a colony was established under, the first settlers suffered hardships as

After Columbus's exploration of the Americas, the Spanish controlled the seas, largely because of their galleons, or large, heavy ships, that looked much like this model. *(Library of Congress, Prints and Photographs Division, [LC-USZ62-103297])*

they tried to build communities in what to them was a wilderness. They also had to deal with the people who were already there.

Native Americans lived in every corner of the Americas. There were vast and complex civilizations in Central and South America. The city that is now known as Cahokia was located along the Mississippi River in what is today Illinois and may have had as many as 50,000 residents. The people of Cahokia built huge earthen mounds that can still be seen today. There has been a lot of speculation as to the total population of Native Americans in 1492. Some have put the number as high as 40 million people.

Most of the early explorers encountered Native Americans. They often wrote descriptions of them for the people of Europe. They also kidnapped a few of these people, took them back to Europe, and put them on display. Despite the number of Native Americans, the Europeans still claimed the land as their own. The rulers of Europe and the Catholic Church at the time felt they had a right to take any lands they wanted from people who did not share their level of technology and who were not Christians.

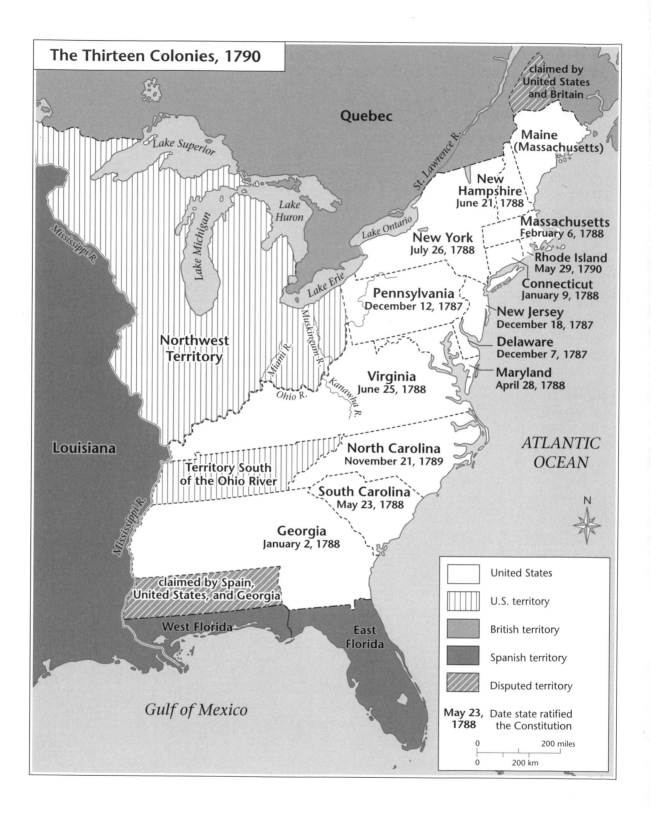

# The Thirteen Colonies, 1790

Quebec

Lake Superior

Lake Michigan

Lake Huron

Mississippi R.

St. Lawrence R.

Lake Ontario

Lake Erie

claimed by United States and Britain

Maine (Massachusetts)

New Hampshire
June 21, 1788

Massachusetts
February 6, 1788

New York
July 26, 1788

Rhode Island
May 29, 1790

Connecticut
January 9, 1788

Pennsylvania
December 12, 1787

New Jersey
December 18, 1787

Delaware
December 7, 1787

Maryland
April 28, 1788

Northwest Territory

Miami R.

Muskingum R.

Ohio R.

Kanawha R.

Virginia
June 25, 1788

Louisiana

North Carolina
November 21, 1789

Territory South of the Ohio River

South Carolina
May 23, 1788

Georgia
January 2, 1788

ATLANTIC OCEAN

N

Mississippi R.

claimed by Spain, United States, and Georgia

West Florida

East Florida

Gulf of Mexico

United States

U.S. territory

British territory

Spanish territory

Disputed territory

May 23, 1788    Date state ratified the Constitution

0          200 miles

0          200 km

# First Contacts

## EARLY EXPLORERS

In the 16th and 17th centuries, the countries of Europe rushed to claim colonies around the world. Often claims to vast territories were based on nothing more than an explorer being the first to see a place. New Jersey ended up an area with conflicting claims from a number of countries, including England, Holland, France, and Sweden.

The first recorded European who may have seen New Jersey was John Cabot, an Italian sponsored by the English, who made two voyages to North America in 1497 and 1498. Like Christopher Columbus, he was looking for a new route to Asia. On his second voyage, Cabot cruised north along the east coast of Greenland. As Cabot sailed into colder and colder regions, his crew became concerned and finally mutinied. Cabot then sailed south to the latitude of Chesapeake Bay. He claimed all the land he sailed along for England.

In 1524, Giovanni da Verrazano, an Italian exploring for the French, was the next European to visit what would become New Jersey. In spring 1524, Verrazano crossed the Atlantic and made his first landfall somewhere along the North Carolina coast. He then sailed north as far as what is now Nova Scotia, exploring the bays and inlets of the coast and making maps. He, too, may have been looking for a passage through or around the continent. Although he failed to find a passage, he established a claim for France that would be a point of conflict between France and England for more than 200 years.

Sponsored by the Dutch East India Company, Henry Hudson sailed the *Half Moon* in 1609. Holland built this replica of the ship in 1909 and donated it to the people of New York for a celebration commemorating the 300th anniversary of Hudson's discovery of the river later named for him. This replica burned in 1931, but a newer replica built in New York was launched in 1989. *(Library of Congress, Prints and Photographs Division [LC-USZ62-72068])*

The Dutch claim to parts of New Jersey was based on the third voyage of Henry Hudson. Hudson had first visited North America in 1607, on a trip sponsored by an English company, and he sailed to the shores of Greenland and the Svalbard islands in search of the Northwest Passage. He made a second voyage in 1608, for the same English company, but this time he tried to sail around the northern tip of Europe looking for a northeast passage to find a shorter route to Asia. When the voyage failed to find a new route, Hudson lost his English supporters.

Hudson then turned to the Dutch East India Company to sponsor his further explorations. Working for the Dutch in the ship the *Half Moon*, Hudson sailed to Nova Scotia and then headed south in hopes he could discover some easier way to get past the North

## Hudson's Fourth Voyage

When Henry Hudson returned to England after his trip to North America that was sponsored by the Dutch, he and his ships were seized by the English authorities. In exchange for his release, he agreed to serve only England in any future voyages. In 1610, a newly formed English company purchased a new ship, the *Discovery,* and hired Hudson to make another trip in search of the Northwest Passage. When he reached Hudson Strait, between the northern tip of eastern Canada and Baffin Island, it was already summer.

Hudson then spent the rest of the summer and well into the fall exploring Hudson Bay. By November, the ice had begun to form in the bay, and the *Discovery* was trapped. During the winter, Hudson and his crew suffered from the cold and a lack of provisions. Being trapped on the ship caused all sorts of problems among the crew, and in June 1611, they mutinied. Hudson, his son, and seven loyal crew members were set adrift in one of the ship's boats. A few of the mutineers finally reached England, and when it was learned what had happened, they were put in prison. Henry Hudson and those who had stayed with him were never heard from again.

Henry Hudson explored in 1609 what would become known as the Hudson River in present-day New York. *(National Archives of Canada)*

American continent. He reportedly believed that the continent was just a narrow isthmus that could be crossed to reach the Pacific Ocean. In September 1609, he sailed into a large bay and decided to explore it. Hudson spent about a month exploring the river that still bears his name.

He and his men traveled about 150 miles up river to the site that would become Albany, New York. Based on Hudson's voyage, the Dutch claimed land in what would become the colonies of New York, Connecticut, and New Jersey. They called this area New Netherland, and the first settlement of the colony was called New Amsterdam, which later became New York City. Dutch settlers from New Amsterdam established Fort Nassau on the Delaware River in 1624. This was the first European settlement in New Jersey. However, before any Europeans arrived, there were between 8,000 and 10,000 Native Americans already living there.

## THE LENNI LENAPE

The Delaware River has been the western boundary of New Jersey since it first became an English colony. The river was named after Lord De La Warr, the first governor of the colony of Virginia. Throughout the watershed of the Delaware River, there lived a group of Native Americans the Europeans called the Delaware Indians. These Native Americans called themselves the Lenni Lenape, which means "the original people." At the time the Europeans arrived, there were approximately 40 different bands of Lenni Lenape who lived in the Delaware River watershed, the lower reaches of the Hudson River, and along the coastal plain of New Jersey.

These people all spoke dialects of the Algonquian language and were divided by language into three distinct groups. The Lenni Lenape in the southern end of the area spoke what are called Southern Unami dialects. The people in the middle of the area spoke Northern Unami-Unalachtigo dialects. In the northern reaches of their territory, the Lenni Lenape groups spoke what are called Munsee dialects.

The Lenni Lenape belonged to the cultural group of Native Americans that anthropologists and ethnographers refer to as Eastern Woodland Indians, or Indians of the Northeast culture area. Like all Woodland Indians at the time, the Lenni Lenape lived in

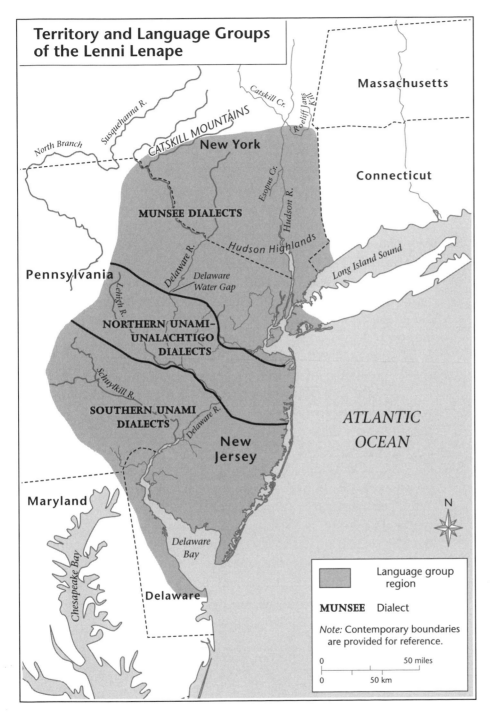

## Territory and Language Groups of the Lenni Lenape

Massachusetts

Catskill Cr.

Roeliff Jans Kill

North Branch

Susquehanna R.

CATSKILL MOUNTAINS

New York

Connecticut

Esopus Cr.

Hudson R.

MUNSEE DIALECTS

Delaware R.

Hudson Highlands

Long Island Sound

Pennsylvania

Delaware Water Gap

Lehigh R.

NORTHERN UNAMI-
UNALACHTIGO
DIALECTS

Schuylkill R.

SOUTHERN UNAMI
DIALECTS

Delaware R.

New
Jersey

ATLANTIC
OCEAN

N

Maryland

Delaware
Bay

Chesapeake Bay

Delaware

| | Language group region |
| --- | --- |
| **MUNSEE** | Dialect |

*Note:* Contemporary boundaries are provided for reference.

0        50 miles

0        50 km

The Lenni Lenape, the Native Americans who lived in New Jersey, were divided into three distinct language dialects. Their language was part of the Algonquian language group.

small bands or groups that depended on farming, hunting, and fishing for their survival. A single band of the Lenni Lenape had three or four places they would live in the course of the year. In the spring and the summer, they lived in an area where they planted their crops. The primary crops of the Lenni Lenape were corn, beans, and a variety of squashes and gourds. Corn was the most important crop. It was the main staple of the Lenni Lenape diet and was prepared in a number of ways. Dried corn and beans were stored and eaten throughout the winter months.

The Lenni Lenape's fields were cleared by burning. When a field lost its fertility, a new area would be burned. In their fields, the Lenni Lenape planted their corn in small hills, and in each hill they planted a few corn seeds. The beans were planted around the corn hills. The cornstalks served as supports for the bean vines. Squash grew between the hills, allowing the Lenni Lenape to maximize the use of the cleared land. In addition to the food crops, the Lenni Lenape, like many other Native American groups, grew small amounts of tobacco for smoking in pipes.

The women of a band were primarily responsible for tending the crops. The Lenni Lenape men spent much of their time hunting and fishing. Fishing in the spring and summer was done in a variety of ways from shore and from the canoes they made by shaping and scraping out a single log. Large weighted nets called seines, which would encircle a school of fish in shallow water, dip nets, hooks and lines, fish traps, and even bows and arrows were used to catch the abundant fish in the rivers, lakes, and bays of the Lenni Lenape territory. A number of shellfish were also gathered by the Lenni Lenape. Near the fishing camps along the New Jersey coast, large mounds of shells accumulated. There are still remnants of these mounds at several locations in New Jersey, including near Barnegat and Tuckerton. Like many Eastern Woodland Indians, the Lenni Lenape used a variety of clamshells to create wampum for jewelry and trade.

Fish and shellfish were usually dried by laying the prepared meat out on racks in the sun. The dried fish would later be added to soups and stews made with the corn, beans, and squash raised in the fields. In addition to fish and shellfish, the Lenni Lenape hunted and ate all sorts of wild game. Deer was the most important game they pursued, and all parts of the animal were used in

## Wampum

The Lenni Lenape, like many other Native American groups along the East Coast of North America, made beads using clamshells. They used a variety of clamshells to create white beads, which were always more plentiful. They used the quahog clamshell to produce dark-colored beads that ranged in color from black to purple and blue. These were more rare. The beads were then strung on leather or hemp twine and fashioned into belts and jewelry.

Much of the wampum was used for decoration, but some wampum belts used a series of symbols that could depict a story or send a message from one group to another. The Native Americans who had access to the coast often traded wampum for goods with other Native Americans in the interior of the continent. Historical accounts of contacts with the Lenni Lenape indicate that they were experts at fashioning elaborate items using wampum.

The colonists soon began to use wampum as money. In the early years of the American colonies, there was little or no money available. At first, people exchanged food as a form of currency, but this had many drawbacks—the major one being its perishable nature. If not consumed, the person accepting the food would soon lose his or her profit. To solve this problem, the colonists began to accept wampum in exchange for goods, and the colonial governments set exchange rates.

In New Netherland, the exchange rate was set at four white beads equaled one stiver. The black or dark beads were worth twice as much. A stiver was the equivalent of an English pence. The last recorded use of wampum as money took place in New York in 1701.

some way. The meat was eaten fresh as well as dried. The hide was used to make clothes. The bones and antlers were used to make a wide variety of tools. The sinew that connects the muscles to the bone was used like string.

Deer were often hunted by large groups of Lenni Lenape working together to drive the deer into large traps where they could be more easily harvested. During these deer drives, the Lenni Lenape often used fire to force the deer in an area to move toward their traps. These communal hunts required the cooperation of several bands of Lenni Lenape. In addition to deer, the Lenni Lenape harvested many other animals.

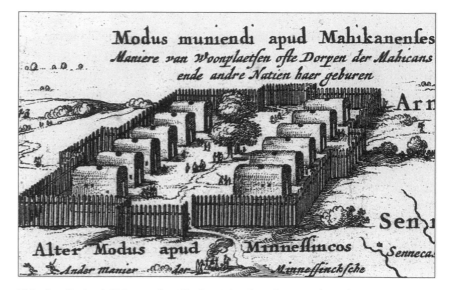

This detail of a 1685 map by Nicolaes Visscher that was based on the explorations of Henry Hudson shows longhouses, the more formal type of shelter the Lenni Lenape used in the winter. *(Library of Congress)*

Moose, bear, and many small animals and birds were hunted or trapped. In the spring, many Lenni Lenape would travel to areas where the now extinct passenger pigeon nested and gather the young birds called squab from the nest. Turkeys were also plentiful in the area of the Lenni Lenape. Turkeys were eaten and their feathers were used by the Lenni Lenape as decoration for their clothing and headdresses.

The Lenni Lenape had two similar types of shelter. At their hunting, fishing, and farming locations, they often built small huts—called wigwams—by placing the ends of saplings (young, flexible trees) in the ground in a circle. The tops of the saplings were then bent into the middle to form a dome. The dome was covered with bark. The floors were covered with woven reed mats. In the winter, the Lenni Lenape tended to live in more formal villages.

The winter villages were often built on the top of a hill and were surrounded by a stockade or palisade made of logs. Inside the stockade, there would be a number of longhouses. A longhouse was also built using saplings, but instead of setting them in a circle, two long rows of saplings would be set. The tops of the saplings were then tied together to form a long, arched frame. The frame was covered with large sections of chestnut-tree bark that were often six feet long. The largest longhouses were more than 100 feet long and twenty feet wide. A longhouse of this size was divided into family sections, and as many as seven to 10 families lived in it. Along the peak of the roof of the longhouse a slot was left to allow the smoke from the cooking fires to escape.

Throughout the winter, the families in a longhouse prepared their meals in large clay pots, and they primarily ate soups and stews. The floors of the longhouse were covered with woven mats. Similar decorated mats covered the walls. Their beds were made from the hides of animals with the fur left on for comfort and warmth. The family sections of the longhouse were divided by partitions, and each family had its own cooking fire. Among the Lenni Lenape, as with many Native American groups, there was very little in the way of private property, and the survival of the band depended on the cooperation of the group.

Because of the communal nature of Native American society, there were numerous misunderstandings when they came into

contact with Europeans. The greatest point of conflict was over land ownership. The Dutch and other early settlers in the area believed in owning the land as individuals and often negotiated with the Lenni Lenape and other local Indians to buy land. At first, neither group spoke the other's language, nor did they understand each other's culture. The Lenni Lenape and other area Indians probably assumed they were agreeing to allow the Europeans to share their land, while the Europeans thought they were buying it. So when Peter Minuit thought he bought Manhattan Island from the Manhattan Indians (a band either of the Lenni Lenape or Wappinger), the Lenni Lenape of the area probably thought he was paying to use it temporarily as they had.

Conflicts between the two groups did not start immediately. At first, the Lenni Lenape were eager to trade with the Europeans for

After arriving in New Netherland in 1626, Peter Minuit bought Manhattan from the Manhattan Indians (part of either the band of Lenni Lenape or the Wappinger) for goods worth 60 guilders. *(Library of Congress)*

## Lenni Lenape Place-names in New Jersey

Many towns in New Jersey have names taken from the Lenni Lenape:

| | | |
|---|---|---|
| Absecon | Lopatcong | Passaic |
| Alloway | Mahway | Rahway |
| Assion | Manalapan | Ramapo |
| Assunpink | Manasquan | Raritan |
| Hackensack | Manunka Chunk | Wanaque |
| Hoboken | Matawan | Watchung |
| Hohokus | Metuchen | Weehawken |
| Hopatcong | Navesink | Wenonah |
| Lenape | Parsippany | Whippany |

metal goods, cloth, and other manufactured items they did not have. The Europeans wanted to get the pelts of various animals, especially beaver, which were in high demand in Europe. As the colonists spread out, they adopted many Lenni Lenape names for places and geographical features of New Jersey that are still used today.

In addition to trading with the Lenni Lenape, the Europeans brought with them diseases that were unknown in North America, and to which the Native Americans had no immunity. Diseases like chicken pox, measles, and smallpox killed many more Lenni Lenape than direct conflict with the colonists ever did. As more and more colonists flooded into the Lenni Lenape territory, armed conflicts arose. Eventually, those Lenni Lenape who survived the fighting and European diseases migrated westward. The remaining Lenni Lenape ended up on reservations in the Midwest and West. Today there is an active group of Native Americans in Oklahoma who consider themselves the descendants of the New Jersey Lenni Lenape.

2

# First Settlements in New Jersey

## DUTCH SETTLERS

Based on Henry Hudson's voyage in 1609, the Dutch claimed a large piece of North America centered on the Hudson River. This included land in what is today New York, Connecticut, Delaware, and New Jersey. The Dutch called their colony New Netherland. At first, no one settled in the colony. Instead, a number of traders arrived at the mouths of the Hudson and Delaware Rivers to buy furs from the Lenni Lenape. One of the trading stops was near Bergen, New Jersey, but no permanent settlement was established.

This changed in 1621, when the Dutch government allowed a group of wealthy merchants to form the Dutch West India Company. The company was created to expand trade with the Native Americans and establish trading posts in New Netherland. Their first settlement, in 1624, was Fort Orange, 150 miles up the Hudson River near what became Albany, New York. In 1625, the company established their second settlement, on Manhattan Island near the mouth of the Hudson River. This second town was called New Amsterdam and is now New York City.

In 1624, Cornelius Mey led a group south to the Delaware River to establish a trading post. It was called Fort Nassau, and it was established on the New Jersey side of the river near present-day Gloucester, New Jersey, and was the first European settlement

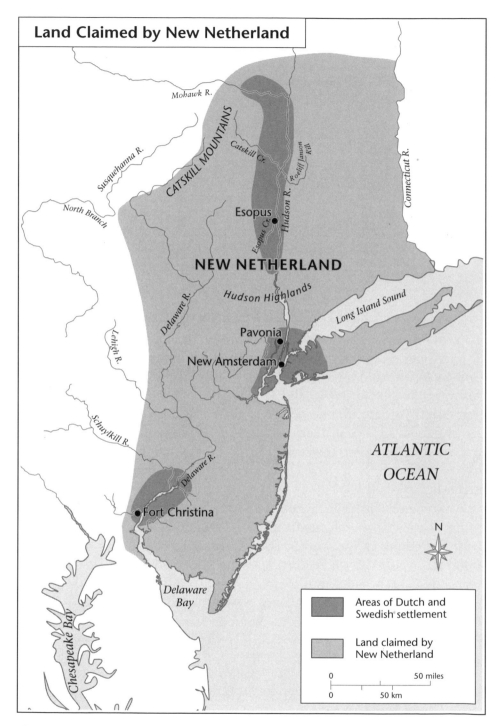

Land Claimed by New Netherland

Mohawk R.

Susquehanna R.

North Branch

CATSKILL MOUNTAINS

Catskill Cr.

Roeliff Janson Kill

Connecticut R.

Esopus Cr.

Hudson R.

Esopus

NEW NETHERLAND

Hudson Highlands

Long Island Sound

Delaware R.

Lehigh R.

Pavonia

New Amsterdam

Schuylkill R.

ATLANTIC OCEAN

Delaware R.

Fort Christina

N

Delaware Bay

Chesapeake Bay

Areas of Dutch and Swedish settlement

Land claimed by New Netherland

0                50 miles

0        50 km

The Dutch claimed all the land between the Connecticut and Delaware Rivers. This land was also claimed by the English, who captured it from the Dutch in 1664.

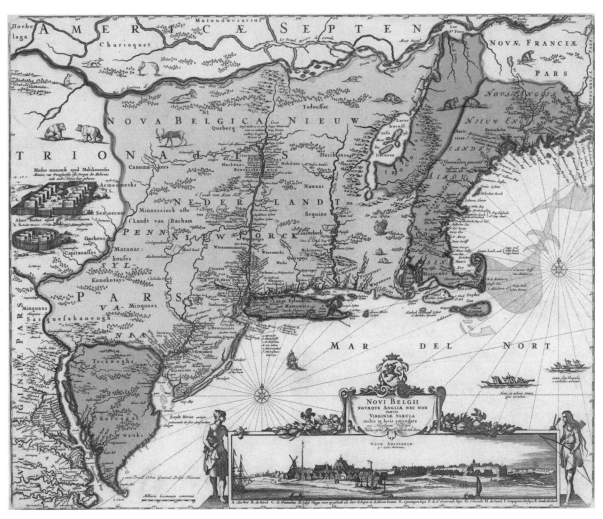

This 17th-century map of New Netherland by Nicolaes Visscher is one of the most well-known of the region. The lower right-hand of the map contains a vignette of New Amsterdam, which would later become New York City. *(Library of Congress, Geography and Map Division)*

in New Jersey. When a Dutch trading ship stopped at Fort Nassau a couple of years later, no one was there. It has never been discovered what happened to the traders who had built the fort. Although no permanent settlement was made at Fort Nassau in 1624, Cape May, the southern tip of New Jersey, was named after Cornelius Mey. Over the years, Fort Nassau was used as a trading post intermittently.

# The Dutch West India Company

In the rush to expand trade with Asia, the Dutch had formed the Dutch East India Company and were highly successful in capturing a large segment of the Asia trade. When Henry Hudson gave them a claim in North America, they tried to duplicate that success by creating the Dutch West India Company in 1621. The company had exclusive rights to set up colonies and conduct trade in the Western Hemisphere. From the beginning, what success it had was much greater in the Caribbean than in New Netherland.

By 1674, the company was in serious financial difficulty and was dissolved. A second Dutch West India Company was created, and after 20 years, it too failed financially. Part of the conflict between the Dutch and the English was caused by the company trading illegally in the English colonies in North America. The Dutch were deeply involved with the tobacco trade in Virginia, as well as with the importation of slaves.

A group of wealthy merchants formed the Dutch West India Company and captured much trade in Asia. Later, the Dutch formed the Dutch East India Company, with which they established New Amsterdam. This engraving shows four Dutch ships off the shore of a small island.
*(Library of Congress, Prints and Photographs Division [LC-USZ62-71452])*

The Van Wagoner homestead, shown in this photograph, is a Dutch settlement located in Passaic County, New Jersey. *(New Jersey Historical Society)*

For a number of reasons, people arrived in New Netherland in very small numbers. At the time, the Netherlands was experiencing economic prosperity, so there was no economic incentive to move to North America. The Netherlands also practiced religious tolerance. Unlike England, where people left so they could freely worship, people came to the Netherlands seeking religious freedom. Another reason potential colonists stayed away from the Dutch colony was its land policies. The Dutch West India Company owned the land and was willing to rent it out to tenant farmers but would not sell it. Many of the people in New Netherland were not Dutch but represented almost all the European nationalities.

Realizing they needed to attract more people to New Netherland, the Dutch created the patroon system. This offered large tracts of land to members of the company who would bring in at least 50 colonists. Michael Pauw, an official with the Dutch West India Company, was granted a patroonship across the Hudson from New Amsterdam in 1630 and called it Pavonia. In 1633, the

This frontispiece from *The new and unknown world, or description of America and the Southland,* a 1671 Dutch book by Arnoldus Montanus, captures the diversity of the various lands the Dutch explored and colonized to different degrees. *(Library of Congress, Rare Book and Special Collections Division)*

## Patroons

Members of the Dutch West India Company who were willing to recruit 50 or more colonists for New Netherland were granted a patroonship. This was a large tract of land in New Netherland that the patroon would own and then rent out to tenant farmers. The patroon system of colonization only had limited success. Most people coming to North America did so seeking the opportunity to own their own farms. The only patroonship in New Jersey was a failure. When the English captured New Netherland in 1664, they allowed a number of patroons in New York to keep their lands. It was not until there were rent riots in 1839 that the patroon system finally ended and many of the tenants were able to purchase the lands they had been renting for many years.

first farm was established in Pavonia near what is today Jersey City. A second home was built nearby shortly thereafter, and then no further development took place. Michael Pauw failed to bring any more settlers to Pavonia, and his claim to the land went back to the company.

In the next several years, a few more families left New Amsterdam and settled in New Jersey, but that soon came to a sudden end. A young Native American who had seen his uncle murdered by a European when he was a child reached an age where he was ready to avenge his relative's death. In the Native American idea of justice at the time, this was an acceptable action. When the young man could not find the actual murderers, he took his revenge by killing a randomly chosen colonist.

The governor of New Netherland, Willem Kieft, did not agree with Native American ideas of justice, and he decided to teach them that they should not kill the colonists. Soldiers from New Amsterdam were sent out to attack any Native Americans they could find on both sides of the Hudson River at night on February 25, 1643. In Pavonia, around 80 Native Americans were killed, including women and children. It was reported that the soldiers threw babies into the Hudson and then shot the parents when they attempted to save their children. Governor Kieft gave the soldiers medals, and set off a war, called Kieft's Indian War, with the Native Americans that was fought sporadically over the next 20 years. Because of the warfare that Kieft had started, all the settlers in New Jersey who did not die in raids by Native Americans moved back to the relative safety of New Amsterdam.

In 1645, the fighting came to a temporary halt when the Dutch signed a peace treaty with the warring Native Americans. After the peace treaty was signed, a few farmers returned to the west bank of the Hudson. These farmers stayed on a narrow strip of land between modern-day Hoboken and Bayonne, New Jersey, where they could easily retreat to New Amsterdam if there were new conflicts with Native Americans in the area. At the same time, traders had once again established a settlement at Fort Nassau.

Settlement in New Jersey progressed slowly as people remained reluctant to move into an area where conflicts with Native Americans were likely. Bergen became the first town in New Jersey in 1660, when the governor of New Netherland, Peter Stuyvesant, had settlers build their houses in a village with a stockade around it.

## NEW SWEDEN

In 1638, yet another country decided to stake a claim to part of North America. Peter Minuit, who had been involved in the establishment of New Netherland, convinced the Swedes that they should get involved in the lucrative fur trade. He also directed them to the Delaware River, which was far enough away from New Amsterdam to the north and Virginia to the south that they would be able to establish a trading colony without interference from either the English or the Dutch.

Although the Swedes went along with Minuit's plan, they were reluctant participants at best. Life was good in Sweden at the time, and very few people were interested in leaving. Some of the people who settled in New Sweden did so only because they were let out of prison early if they agreed to go to North America as colonists.

The first Swedish settlement was Fort Christina at what is now Wilmington, Delaware. Under the direction of Governor Johan Printz, the Swedes built a number of small forts along the Delaware

River, including Fort Nya Elfsborg. This fort was south of Fort Christina on the eastern shore of Delaware near what is now Salem, New Jersey. It was not very far from the Dutch Fort Nassau. It was reported to be a miserable place and was given the nickname *Muggenborg*, which means "mosquito town." It was abandoned in 1651. The population of New Sweden never reached 500 people.

## THE FIGHT FOR NEW JERSEY

In 1654, Peter Stuyvesant received orders from his employers in the Netherlands: He was to take whatever army he could raise and take over New Sweden. It was an easy task, as the Dutch were able to put together an expedition with more soldiers than there were people in New Sweden. When Stuyvesant showed up at Fort Christina with seven ships and between 500 and 800 men, the Swedes surrendered without a shot being fired. Many of the Swedes returned to Europe. Those who remained were soon swallowed up by the influx of English colonists. The English had never recognized either the Dutch or the Swedish claims in North America and were soon in control of the East Coast from Maine to Georgia.

Peter Stuyvesant arrived in New Netherland in 1647 and governed the colony until his 1664 surrender to the English. *(Delaware Public Archives, Dover, Delaware)*

# 3

# The English in New Jersey

England went through a period of social and political disruption in the middle of the 17th century. The Puritans in England revolted against King Charles I and overthrew him in 1649. Oliver Cromwell, the leader of the Puritans, became Lord Protector, and was the leader of England until his death in 1658. Upon Cromwell's death, his son took over briefly before Charles I's son returned to England, and the monarchy was restored under the rule of Charles II. After years in exile, the people who had been loyal to Charles II returned to England, and the king wanted to reward them.

Many received new titles and positions in the king's government. Others received large grants of land in North America. One of the largest grants of land went to Charles II's brother, James, duke of York. James was given all the land between the Connecticut River and the Delaware River.

## JAMES, DUKE OF YORK, LORD PROPRIETOR OF NEW YORK AND NEW JERSEY

While in exile, James, duke of York, had served in the Spanish military in their war against Puritan England. On his return, when his brother became king, James was made lord high admiral of England, which put him in charge of the most powerful navy in the world at the time. Although his brother had given him lands in

# James, Duke of York, later King James II
## (1633–1701)

In 1649, King Charles I was removed from the throne and executed after a Puritan revolution in England. His two sons, Charles, prince of Wales, and James, duke of York, were forced to spend the next eight years living in exile while the Puritan Oliver Cromwell ran England. Charles lived in poverty in the Netherlands and James went to Spain, where he joined the Spanish navy in its war against Protestant England. When the English monarchy was restored in 1660, James's older brother became Charles II, king of England.

Charles II appointed James lord high admiral of the navy and in 1664 granted James all the lands between the Connecticut and Delaware Rivers in North America. James sent a fleet to capture the territory claimed by the Dutch and was involved with the fate of New York and New Jersey for the next 24 years.

In 1672, James created a controversy by revealing that he had converted to Catholicism. Although England tolerated many different Protestant sects, the country was not tolerant of Catholics. In fact, in 1673, Parliament passed a series of laws called the Tests Acts, which barred Catholics from holding office. James was forced to resign his position as lord high admiral.

Because his brother had not produced an heir, James was next in line to become king of England. On his brother's death in 1685, many tried to block James from becoming king. However, they were unsuccessful and he became James II, king of England.

As king, he was faced with a number of uprisings in England. He was extremely brutal in addressing any resistance to his rule. He was so unpopular that, in 1688, he was removed from the throne in a bloodless coup known as the Glorious Revolution. After a brief and unsuccessful attempt to regain his throne, he spent the rest of his life living in exile in France.

James II, as shown in this early-19th-century engraving, ruled England for only four years—1685 to 1688. *(Library of Congress, Prints and Photographs Division [LC-USZ62-92123])*

Peter Stuyvesant governed the Dutch colony of New Amsterdam (later New York City) until his surrender on September 8, 1664, to an English force led by Colonel Richard Nicolls. *(Library of Congress, Prints and Photographs Division [LC-USZ62-84401])*

North America, there was an obstacle to his claim. The lands he had been granted were the same territory that the Dutch considered theirs as New Netherland.

At the time, there was a lot of competition between the Dutch and the English for control of trade around the world. In North America, with the exception of Florida, the English controlled the East Coast, from Charleston, Carolina (it was one colony at the time), to the northern end of Maine, which was part of Massachusetts. In the middle of this was New Netherland. George II and James wanted to solidify England's lands in North America. As the head of the navy, James sent a fleet of ships to capture New Netherland.

The fleet was under the command of Colonel Richard Nicolls. Nicolls and his fleet arrived in Boston in August 1664 and then sailed south to the Hudson River. The Dutch governor, Peter Stuyvesant, wanted to fight despite the superiority of the English forces. However, a number of people in New Amsterdam signed a petition against fighting the English. On September 8, 1664, Stuyvesant surrendered and signed New Netherland over to Nicolls.

New Netherland became New York in honor of the duke. New Amsterdam's name was also changed, and it became New York City. By the end of the month, the English flag flew over the entire colony, including outposts at Albany and on the Delaware River. Richard Nicolls assumed the position of royal governor of New York.

## ENGLISH SETTLEMENT

A number of groups had been blocked from moving to the west bank of the Hudson by Stuyvesant. Many of these people were English colonists from New England and Long Island. They petitioned Nicolls for permission to move to what would soon be New Jersey, and he granted them the right to settle there.

Once they had permission to move into the territory granted them by Nicolls, the settlers had to acquire rights to the land from the Lenni Lenape in the area. One of the first groups into the area at this time received the right to settle a section of land between the Passaic and the Raritan Rivers and extending 30 miles inland. For this huge piece of land, they paid the Lenni Lenape 400 fathoms of wampum and an assortment of trade goods. This included cloth, coats, other clothing, gunpowder, rifles, and lead. These settlers established the first English town in New Jersey and called it Elizabethtown (later shortened to Elizabeth), which was reportedly named after Sir George Carteret's wife, Elizabeth.

Within a short period of time, five more new towns were established by a number of groups, most of whom were seeking religious and personal freedoms. Quakers from Long Island and Baptists from Rhode Island received the right to settle a 12-mile-wide tract that ran from south of Raritan Bay to Sandy Hook. They established the towns of Shrewbury and Middletown.

# The Early Settlers

Before 1664, a group of Puritans who had moved from New England to Long Island were looking for a new place to settle. They thought the land on Long Island was too sandy and not well suited to farming. This group entered into negotiations with the Dutch governor, Peter Stuyvesant, for land in what would become New Jersey. When Colonel Nicolls sailed into the mouth of the Hudson River and took over New Amsterdam, these same Puritans were the first people to ask for the right to settle on the west bank of the Hudson.

This group, and those who followed from Connecticut, Massachusetts, and New Hampshire, came to take advantage of the unsettled land of New Jersey. They brought with them the New England tradition of town meetings and self-government. This put them in conflict with the ideas of government and property ownership outlined in the Concession and Agreement that set up the rules and laws for New Jersey.

Their Puritan ideals and New England traditions, coupled with conflicts over their land claims granted by Governor Nicolls before the New Jersey proprietorship was known, colored relations in the colony throughout the colonial period. There would be a strong division between those who came to New Jersey from other English colonies seeking land and religious toleration, and those who profited from their participation in the proprietary form of government. When the American Revolution came to New Jersey, these two groups divided into Patriots seeking independence and Loyalists who supported England and the king.

Next, the Elizabethtown Associates, as they were called, sold off half their land to a group of Puritans from New England. They established two more towns, Woodbridge and Piscataway. Nicolls made a third grant to another group of Puritans who came from the area of New Haven, Connecticut. They were led by Robert Treat. Their territory was bordered by the Passaic River, the Watchung Mountains, and Newark Bay. Their new town was named Newark.

In a very short time, the west bank of the Hudson River went from having one Dutch town at Bergen to seven communities. The new settlements were almost immediately plunged into conflict when it was learned that James had kept New York for himself and granted all the land between the Hudson and Delaware Rivers to two of his and his brother's loyal supporters, Sir George Carteret and Lord John Berkeley. Carteret had been governor of the Isle of Jersey, an English possession in the English Channel, and had remained loyal to the king. It was in honor of Carteret's island home that New Jersey received its name.

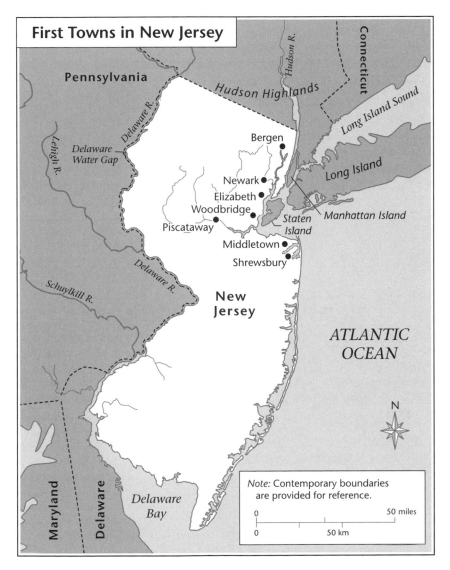

**First Towns in New Jersey**

The Dutch settlement of Bergen was the first town in New Jersey. When the English captured New Netherland in 1664, six towns founded by people from other colonies were quickly established.

## Sir George Carteret
### (ca. 1610–1680)

When the monarchy was restored in 1660, and Charles II became king, he rewarded many of the people who had been loyal to his father and had been in exile during the reign of Cromwell and the Puritans. Sir George Carteret had been in the navy, and Charles I had made him comptroller of the navy in 1639 and then lieutenant governor of the Isle of Jersey, in the English Channel, for his service to the king during the English Revolution. In 1651, Carteret was forced to leave Jersey and live in exile. He joined the French navy in its fight against Puritan England.

When the monarchy was restored and Charles II became king, Carteret returned to England and was rewarded with a number of important positions. One of the jobs he was given was treasurer for the navy. He gave up this job in 1667 when there were problems with the navy's accounts.

Carteret was also involved in two colonies. He was one of the original proprietors of the Carolina colony in 1663 and was made co-proprietor of New Jersey with John, Lord Berkeley. In 1676, when Berkeley sold his half of the colony, Carteret became the sole proprietor of East New Jersey.

## CONCESSION AND AGREEMENT OF THE LORD PROPRIETORS OF THE PROVINCE OF NEW JERSEY

When John, Lord Berkeley and Sir George Carteret received all the lands between the Hudson and the Delaware Rivers from James, Duke of York, they drew up an official document on the rights they had over the land and the rights they granted to any colonists. This document is called the Concession and Agreement of the Lord Proprietors of the Province of New Caesarea, or New Jersey, to and With All and Every the Adventurers and All Such as Shall Settle or Plant There—1664.

Under the Concession and Agreement, New Jersey was to be ruled by a governor appointed by the Proprietors John, Lord Berkeley and Sir George Carteret. The governor would allow the residents of the colony to elect a general assembly. Under these rules, women were allowed to be freeholders along with the men.

New Jersey was the first colony to do this. A major problem arose over land ownership. The Dutch in Bergen and those in the grants made by Nicolls believed they owned their land.

According to the Concession and Agreement, all land was owned by the proprietors, and settlers were supposed to pay rent. This created a number of conflicts between the settlers who moved in immediately after Nicolls captured New Netherland and the government of the Lord Proprietors. Berkeley and Carteret sent Carteret's 26 year-old nephew, Captain Philip Carteret, as the governor of New Jersey.

Philip Carteret arrived in New Jersey at Elizabethtown with his wife and a small band of settlers and made it the first capital of New Jersey. To smooth things over with the Elizabethtown associates, Carteret bought out one of the six original associates. For the first few years, everything went fairly well. But in 1670, the first "quit rents," as they were called, came due. Those who held their lands from the grants made by Nicolls felt they did not have to pay. Carteret felt otherwise and tried to collect.

The two sides argued for two years, and then in 1672, the situation came to a crisis. The members of the General Assembly courted the favor of Captain James Carteret, the governor's son and heir who had recently arrived in the colony. They then overthrew the governor and elected James Carteret the president of

Nephew of George Carteret; co-proprietor of New Jersey with John, Lord Berkeley; Philip Carteret arrived in the colony as its first governor in 1665. *(Library of Congress)*

New Jersey. Philip Carteret returned to England to consult with his uncle and Berkeley.

When the duke of York heard about the "rent revolt" in New Jersey, he took immediate action. He declared the land grants of Nicolls null and void. Anyone in New Jersey who did not receive a new patent on their land would lose it. It was further stated that anyone who did not have a new patent could not vote or hold office. This ended the rent revolt, but it set the stage for later protests against English authority in the colony.

# Life in Colonial New Jersey

While Carteret was still in England, a Dutch fleet sailed into New York harbor in July 1673 and recaptured the colony. For more than a year, New Jersey was once again ruled by the Dutch. However, it was returned to its English proprietors by treaty in November 1674. Under the Dutch, the approximately 2,500 citizens of New Jersey were left on their own. When Carteret returned as governor, there was increasing confusion and resentment over land ownership in the colony.

Unknown to the people in the colony, John, Lord Berkeley experienced financial difficulties. To raise money, he sold his half of New Jersey to a group of Quakers. At first, James, duke of York, refused to recognize the deal. When he did, New Jersey was divided in half. Sir George Carteret remained the proprietor of East New Jersey. The Quakers began to make plans to establish their own colony in the mostly uninhabited section of West New Jersey. New Jersey remained divided until 1702.

## THE GROWTH OF THE COLONY

East New Jersey grew rapidly in the last quarter of the 17th century. Sir George Carteret died in 1681. His share of New Jersey was put up for auction by his wife, Elizabeth Carteret. William Penn and 11 other Englishmen bought the colony of East New Jersey for £3,400. Penn and his associates then sold half of their interest to

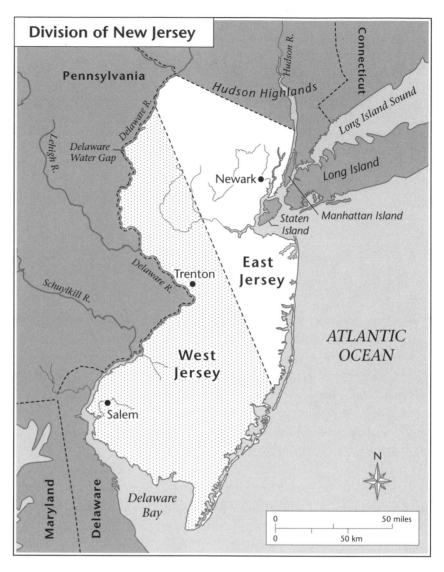

**Division of New Jersey**

Pennsylvania

Hudson R.

Connecticut

Hudson Highlands

Long Island Sound

Delaware R.

Lehigh R.

Delaware Water Gap

Newark •

Long Island

Manhattan Island

Staten Island

**East Jersey**

Schuylkill R.

Delaware R.

Trenton •

ATLANTIC OCEAN

**West Jersey**

Salem •

N

Maryland

Delaware

Delaware Bay

0          50 miles

0          50 km

When John, Lord Berkeley sold his half-interest in the colony of New Jersey in 1667, the colony was divided into East and West New Jersey. The colony was rejoined in 1702, when it became a royal colony.

12 Scots. There were now 24 proprietors who had a share in East New Jersey. Only one of these speculators moved to New Jersey. Many of the others split their holdings into pieces and sold them to people who wanted to move to the colony. These "resident

# The Society of Friends

Around 1647, an English lay minister named George Fox started preaching that he believed that everyone had an "inner light" that was the manifestation of Christ. He preached that all people were capable of finding "Christ within" on their own without the help of a minister or priest. Fox did not intend to start a new religious group, but his ideas attracted many people who formed into a Society of Friends. These groups met for religious purposes, and members were often observed trembling as they had moments where they claimed to be in touch with their inner light. From this, the group gained the nickname Quakers.

The Quakers developed many beliefs that put them in opposition to the Church of England and the government. In addition to their meetings, which were illegal, Quakers refused to swear oaths of allegiance, pay tithes or contributions to the Church of England, and fight in the military. At one point, there were more than 1,500 Quakers in prison in England because of their beliefs.

William Penn and other Quakers began coming to North America in the 1660s, and in some places such as Massachusetts, they faced the same type of persecution they had experienced in England. Roger Williams's colony in Rhode Island was one of the few places they were made welcome until they were able to found their own colonies. In 1674, prominent Quakers led by William Penn were able to purchase John, Lord Berkeley's half of New Jersey and set up a Quaker colony there known as West New Jersey. Penn was granted additional lands in 1681, which became the colony of Pennsylvania. In a short period of time, more than 7,000 Quakers had moved to West New Jersey and Pennsylvania.

The Society of Friends, also known as Quakers, traces it roots to George Fox's preaching about an "inner light" that all people have. Fox claimed it was the manifestation of Christ in each person. This early 19th-century watercolor shows a traveler's interpretation of a Quaker. *(National Archives of Canada)*

# Slavery in New Jersey

There is no record of when the first enslaved Africans arrived in New Jersey. However, the Dutch were prominent in the slave trade and are known to have had slaves from the very beginning. Therefore, it is likely there were slaves in New Jersey's earliest settlements of Pavonia and Fort Nassau. When the English took over New Netherland in 1664, there was a land bonus of 60 extra acres for each slave a settler brought to the colony.

There was always an active slave auction in New Amsterdam that continued when the settlement became New York City. There was also a smaller slave auction in Perth Amboy, New Jersey. Most of the slaves brought into New Jersey came via the Caribbean. The market for slaves in New Jersey was not large enough to absorb a shipload of slaves directly from Africa. New Jersey had a Slave Code, a series of laws that

The Dutch were one of the European empires involved in the transatlantic slave trade during the 17th century. In 1637, as shown in this illustration from a 1671 Dutch book, they captured Elmina, a fort on the coast of West Africa, from which they transported slaves to their sugar plantations in Brazil. *(Library of Congress, Rare Book and Special Collections Division)*

proprietors" often brought indentured servants with them and cleared large estates, many of them with more than 1,000 acres. This was at a time when most of the other settlers in East New Jersey had small farms of between 100 and 200 acres.

governed the keeping of slaves. From the time New Jersey became an English colony through the end of the colonial period, the slave populations made up between 6 percent and 8 percent of the total population of the colony.

There were always more male slaves than female slaves in New Jersey, and most of them worked in the fields, although there were a number of male slaves who worked as blacksmiths, carpenters, coopers, tanners, and millwrights. Most of the female slaves worked as domestic servants or in the fields.

Slaves who showed any attempts at rebellion or who committed crimes against whites were treated harshly. In 1695, three black slaves were convicted of murdering their owner. Two of them were hanged, and the third was burned alive. There were other instances of slaves being burned as punishment for crimes. Others were flogged, and at least one slave who was part of a suspected rebellion had his ear cut off.

On the issue of slavery, East and West Jersey disagreed. The Quakers of West New Jersey were opposed to slavery, and there were very few slaves in that part of the colony. In fact, the abolition movement in the United States began with the Quakers of New Jersey and Pennsylvania. The large estates that existed in East New Jersey frequently depended on slave labor, especially when the economic situation in Europe improved and very few indentured servants arrived in the colony.

When the War for Independence came, it had an impact on slavery in New Jersey. Slaves were allowed to join both the Continental and British armies. Those who fought in the war were promised their freedom. The slaves who joined the British forces, for the most part, left with the British at the end of the war.

In 1786, New Jersey made the slave trade illegal. Slavery would become a major issue in the first half of the 19th century, as many in the North agreed with the sentiments expressed on July 4, 1783, by Moses Bloomfield of Woodbridge when he freed his 14 slaves. He said:

*As a nation we are free and independent—all men are created equal—and why should these, my fellow citizens, my equals, be held in bondage? From this day they are emancipated, and I hereby declare them free and absolve them of all servitude to me, or my posterity.*

The Scottish investors wanted to create a new Scotland in New Jersey. Scotland was experiencing a time of religious intolerance, and the investors felt many people would be eager to immigrate to New Jersey. Four hundred Scots came to New Jersey. They were

Built in 1726, the building in this 1936 photograph served as a meeting house for the Society of Friends, or Quakers, in Princeton, New Jersey.
*(Library of Congress, Prints and Photographs Division [HABS-NJ, II-PRINT, 5-I])*

## Farming in Colonial New Jersey

New Jersey has become one of the most densely populated states in the country, but it is still known as "the Garden State." The colonists who came to New Jersey found it to have a moderate climate with rich, deep soil. Many crops were successfully grown in the early days of New Jersey, including barley, corn, oats, and wheat. They also were able to grow numerous vegetables. Livestock also flourished on the pastures of New Jersey. The practice of raising racehorses began during the colonial period and became so much a part of the life of New Jerseyans that there is a head of a racehorse on the state seal.

Many of the farms in New Jersey were relatively small, averaging approximately 100 acres. At the same time, there were huge estates of more than 1,000 acres that were worked by tenant farmers or, in some cases, slaves.

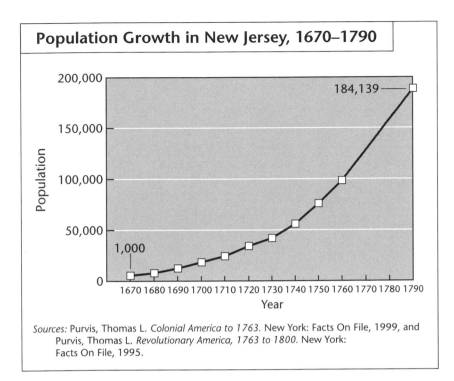

## Population Growth in New Jersey, 1670–1790

184,139

1,000

Year

Population

200,000

150,000

100,000

50,000

0

1670 1680 1690 1700 1710 1720 1730 1740 1750 1760 1770 1780 1790

*Sources:* Purvis, Thomas L. *Colonial America to 1763.* New York: Facts On File, 1999, and Purvis, Thomas L. *Revolutionary America, 1763 to 1800.* New York: Facts On File, 1995.

Once New Jersey became an English colony, it saw rapid and continuous growth throughout the colonial period.

mostly Presbyterians who brought even more diversity to the makeup of the colony.

There was also a group of planters from the island of Barbados who bought huge tracts of land in East New Jersey. The first purchase was more than 15,000 acres, and it was located between the Hackensack and Passaic Rivers. Other Barbadian purchases followed. Some of these purchases were made as land speculation. Others were settled by Barbadians who brought slaves with them to work the land.

In West New Jersey, the population also grew rapidly. However, unlike the diversity in East New Jersey, the western half of the colony was settled primarily by English Quakers. The first settlement of Quakers was at Salem. Their leader was John Fenwick. They immediately ran into problems because the land transactions had not been finalized in England. Fenwick's colony at Salem was followed by a larger group that established the town at Burlington. William Penn, who would soon found the Quaker

# William Penn
## (1644–1718)

William Penn, who was involved in the colonies of East and West New Jersey and Pennsylvania, was the son of British admiral William Penn. His mother, Margaret, was the daughter of a Dutch merchant. Penn attended Christ Church College at Oxford University in England until he was expelled in 1662 for criticizing the Church of England. He traveled in Europe for a while and then was sent to Ireland in 1666 to oversee the family estates in County Cork. While in Ireland, he declared himself to be a Quaker.

In Ireland, his beliefs once again got him in trouble, and he was imprisoned briefly. When he returned to England, he wrote a religious tract entitled, *The Sandy Foundation Shaken.* This time, Penn ended up in the Tower of London, one of England's most famous prisons. In 1669, while in prison, he wrote *No Cross, No Crown* and *Innocency With Her Open Eyes.* Both works dealt with his Quaker beliefs, and he became one of the leading spokespeople for the Society of Friends.

When his father died in 1670, William Penn inherited his father's substantial fortune and estates. He used his new resources to first invest in West New Jersey, where he helped write the colony's very liberal Concession and Agreement, and then in East New Jersey after Sir George Carteret died. In addition to money and property, William Penn inherited a debt that was owed to his father by Charles II, king of England. By 1680, with the accumulation of interest, the debt owed Penn had grown to £16,000. As payment for this debt, Charles II granted Penn a large tract of land in North America in March 1681 that was named Pennsylvania in his honor.

Although Penn spent only four years in the colony, 1682–84 and 1699–1701, Pennsylvania grew rapidly and became the population center for the Quakers in North America.

After receiving a charter from King Charles II, William Penn informed Native Americans inhabiting the area that would become Pennsylvania of his intentions to establish an English colony there. *(Library of Congress, Prints and Photographs Division [LC-USZ62-2583])*

haven of Pennsylvania, was one of the investors in this group as well as in East New Jersey.

Although Penn's own colony became the primary center of the Society of Friends in North America, West New Jersey grew rapidly. The people of the western part of the colony traded along the Delaware River and soon turned to Philadelphia as their commercial and social center. The people in East New Jersey looked to New York City. This is a division that many contend continues today.

In 1670, the estimated population of New Jersey was about 1,000 people. With all the different schemes and promoters in East and West New Jersey, there were more than 14,000 people there by 1700. By the first official U.S. census in 1790, the state of New Jersey had more than 184,000 people.

## POLITICAL TURMOIL IN NEW JERSEY

The diverse beliefs, land-ownership arrangements, and varied places of origin for the people of New Jersey created great political turmoil. Dividing the colony created two separate colonial governments. Then, events in England forced even greater changes to the government. Mostly what the people of New Jersey wanted was the chance to work their farms and have the religious and personal freedoms that had been promised to them under the original Concession and Agreement.

There were so many different groups in New Jersey that conflicts could not be avoided. The various proprietors were often interested in trying to turn a profit. Settlers wanted to own the lands that they improved as they cleared and planted their farms. There were also serious problems between New Jersey and Edmund Andros, who was the appointed governor of New York.

Andros's contention was that his authority superceded that of Governor Phillip Carteret and the government in West New Jersey. He successfully collected customs duties on goods entering the Delaware River. When he tried to do the same with goods bound for East New Jersey that entered via the Hudson River, Carteret and the merchants of East Jersey resisted.

Andros was a man of action, and he took a force of soldiers across the Hudson and arrested Governor Carteret. Carteret was

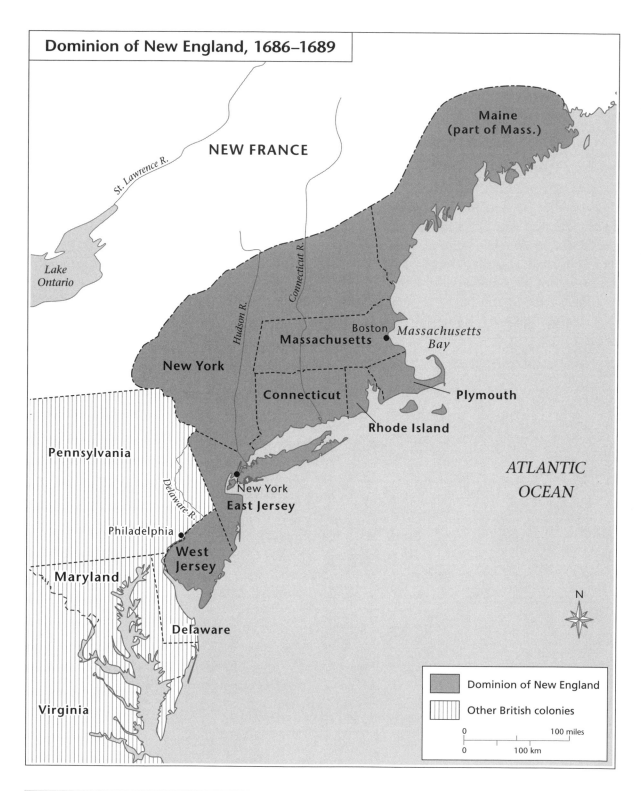

## Dominion of New England, 1686–1689

NEW FRANCE

*St. Lawrence R.*

*Lake Ontario*

Maine (part of Mass.)

*Connecticut R.*

*Hudson R.*

**New York**

Boston

**Massachusetts**

*Massachusetts Bay*

**Connecticut**

**Plymouth**

**Rhode Island**

**Pennsylvania**

New York

**East Jersey**

*Delaware R.*

Philadelphia

**West Jersey**

**Maryland**

**Delaware**

**Virginia**

*ATLANTIC OCEAN*

N

Dominion of New England

Other British colonies

| 0 | 100 miles |
| 0 | 100 km |

put on trial in New York, but he was acquitted by a jury. Back in East Jersey, the members of the General Assembly saw this as a sign of the governor's weakness and continued to resist his leadership. The rule of the proprietors soon ended.

In 1685, James, duke of York, became James II, king of England, Scotland, and Ireland. As king, James II decided to change the way that England ruled its colonies. In 1686, his first move was to combine the troublesome New England colonies into one royal administrative unit, called the Dominion of New England. In 1688, James II added New York and New Jersey into the Dominion of New England. Sir Edmund Andros was appointed governor of this one colony, which included all the lands and people from New Jersey north to the boundary between Maine and Canada.

During the next four years, near anarchy reigned in New Jersey. The proprietors asserted that their rights of ownership could not be taken away from them. Some tried to use this time of chaos to evict people who were living on grants made by Governor Nicolls. There were riots outside of courts in East New Jersey, while in the courts of London, the very legality of the proprietorships was being questioned.

James II was ousted as king in 1688 and was replaced by his oldest daughter, Mary, and her husband, William of Orange. William and Mary were concerned with the pressing needs of

William III, prince of Orange, ruled England, Scotland, and Ireland jointly with Mary II, daughter of James II, from 1689 until Mary's death in 1694. Afterward, William III ruled alone until 1702. This illustration shows him at the 1690 Battle of the Boyne, in which his Protestant forces defeated James II's Catholic forces. *(Library of Congress, Prints and Photographs Division [LC-USZ62-54812])*

*Opposite page:* From 1688 to 1689, New Jersey was part of the Dominion of New England, which combined New Jersey, New York, Connecticut, Rhode Island, Massachusetts (which included Maine), and New Hampshire into one royal colony.

Andrew Hamilton governed both East and West New Jersey. *(Library of Congress, Prints and Photographs Division [LC-USZ62-70245])*

defending the American colonies against the French in Canada and their Native American allies. New York was critical in this defense because of its shared frontier with French Canada. The first plan was to unite New Jersey and New York under one governor. However, the remaining proprietors of both New Jerseys convinced the king and queen to allow a separate governor to oversee the two halves of New Jersey. Andrew Hamilton had served in a number of colonial posts, and in 1692, he became the governor of both East and West New Jersey, which continued to have separate assemblies.

In 1702, James II's second daughter, Anne, became queen of England. She and her advisers decided it was time to end the rule of the proprietors. On April 15, 1702, they joined the two New Jerseys into one royal colony and created other royal colonies throughout English North America. This meant that the colonies were now under the control of the Crown and its appointees. This made the administration of all the colonies more uniform.

Although some self-government remained at the lower levels of government, the people of New Jersey were upset by the shift of power from the colony to London. Queen Anne and her advisers thought they were solving serious problems with the colonies, but they were in fact setting the stage for the American rebellion.

*Opposite page:* Daughter of James II, Anne II was queen of Great Britain and Ireland from 1702 until her death in 1714. This engraving is from a statue of the leader at Blenheim Palace in Woodstock, England. *(Library of Congress, Prints and Photographs Division [LC-USZ62-110255])*

The appointment of Edward Hyde, Lord Cornbury as governor of both New York and New Jersey caused even more problems for the royal colony of New Jersey. Cornbury and his followers were much more interested in personal profit than they were in good government. The group became known as "The Cornbury Ring." They stacked the regional governments of East and West Jersey with people who were a part of the ring or willing to go along with their plots for their own benefit.

The Cornbury Ring profited through shady land deals, illegal taxes, and laws aimed at persecuting the Quakers. Cornbury regularly switched sides between the various New Jersey factions, depending on who paid him the largest bribe. Although he was a cousin of Queen Anne, even she finally had enough and recalled him to England in 1708. For the next 30 years, the colony continued its internal arguments under a succession of governors shared with New York.

Finally, in 1738, Lewis Morris, a wealthy landowner in both New Jersey and New York, convinced the Crown it was time for

## Edward Hyde, Lord Cornbury
### (1661–1723)

When it was learned that New Jersey would become a royal colony in 1702, most saw it as good news. That was before they had any experience with the first royal governor, Lord Cornbury, who governed both New Jersey and New York. Even Queen Anne is reported to have said, before she recalled him to England, that even though he was closely related to her, he should not be protected "in oppressing her subjects."

Throughout his term as governor of New York and New Jersey, there were numerous scandals about his greed and illegal dealings. It was said that he used his post almost exclusively to increase his own wealth. His support was always available to the highest bidder, and he was often known to switch sides in the middle of a controversy when the opposing side came up with a bigger bribe. Many people also found his personal life questionable. When his wife died in 1706, he reportedly showed up at her funeral dressed as a woman.

## Lewis Morris
### (1671–1746)

Lewis Morris was born in Morrisania, which is now part of the Bronx, New York. He had large land holdings in both New York and New Jersey and believed in the aristocratic traditions of England. Many people have reported that he always felt he knew better than the people what New Jersey needed. Morris was extremely active in New Jersey politics and was one of the resident proprietors. When it became obvious that the time of the proprietorships were coming to an end, he went to London and took a lead role in negotiating the transition to a royal colony. He served in the General Assembly of East Jersey and was appointed to the governor's council when New Jersey became a royal colony.

When New Jersey finally became a royal colony, it was lumped with New York, and the two colonies shared one governor. For the next 35 years, Lewis Morris lobbied London to separate New Jersey and New York. In 1738, he was finally successful. New Jersey became a separate colony and Morris was rewarded for his efforts by becoming its first governor, a position he held until his death in 1746.

New Jersey to have its own governor. Morris became the governor and served until 1746. Although Morris was a popular leader for many years in New Jersey before becoming governor, he was always very much a Loyalist and supported the decisions of the Crown. As such, he often found himself in conflict with the people of New Jersey and their elected assembly who were, like many colonists, interested in more freedom for themselves and less control from London.

# 5

# Road to Revolution

Between 1689 and 1763, four wars were fought between the French and English over land in North America. In the final war, known in North America as the French and Indian War and in Europe as the Seven Years' War (1754–63), more than 1,000 New Jersey militiamen fought along with the British regulars. Although there were no battles fought in New Jersey, a small number of people were killed by Native Americans who were allies of the French Canadians. When the conflict between France and England was finally settled by the Treaty of Paris in 1763, officials in London decided it was time to make the colonies pay their share of the costs of the war. Although the groundwork for revolution had been laid from the very beginning, it was a series of laws passed by the Parliament in London that would bring the situation between London and its colonies in North America to war.

## THE SUGAR ACT

Throughout the first half of the 18th century, the Crown had tried a number of laws and regulations to control and tax trade in the colonies. It was in England's best interest to keep the colonies from exporting manufactured goods that competed with the factories of England. At the same time, they wanted exclusive access to the raw materials and agricultural goods that were coming out of the colonies. For the most part, the early attempts at controlling colonial trade had failed. People either ignored them completely or found ways to work around them.

In 1764, Parliament amended the Molasses Act of 1733 with the Sugar and Molasses Act of 1764. The earlier act had tried to exclude molasses not produced in British colonies from being imported into the colonies. The colonies of New England were the primary merchants in the sugar and molasses trade with the Caribbean. However, these laws applied to and affected merchants in New Jersey.

The one part of the 1764 act that affected everyone in all the colonies in North America was the provision that strengthened the role of the customs agents in American ports. Up until this point, customs agents had been ineffective at collecting import and export duties. The Sugar Act made the colonists aware that Parliament and the British government believed they could tax the colonies without their consent.

## THE STAMP ACT

Other than upsetting the people in the colonies, the new Sugar Act did little to raise revenue for the Crown in the colonies. The reaction of Parliament was to pass the Stamp Act in 1765. The Stamp Act required that all legal documents, newspapers, and many consumer goods have a tax stamp attached to them before they were filed or sold. The people of New Jersey and the other colonies did not wait for the stamps to arrive from England. They began protesting as soon as knowledge of the Stamp Act reached the colony.

In New Jersey, as in other colonies, people organized to protest the Stamp Act. These patriotic groups were known as the "Sons of Liberty," and the phrase "no taxation without representation" rang out from Georgia in the South all the way up the coast to New Hampshire and Massachusetts. In New Jersey, the Sons of Liberty pressured the stamp agent, William Coxe, into quitting before any stamps were ever issued. In fact,

When affixed to goods, this stamp signified that a tax must be paid upon purchase. Many colonists felt that the British unfairly introduced these taxes when they implemented the Stamp Act in 1765, which affected goods ranging from business transactions to playing cards. *(Library of Congress, Prints and Photographs Division [LC-USZ61-539])*

## Sons of Liberty

When the Stamp Act was passed in Parliament in 1765, people in the colonies formed groups in their communities to protest the act. One of the opponents of the Stamp Act in the House of Commons, Issac Barré, called the protestors the "sons of liberty." Soon the name spread to the colonies, where it was readily adopted. It was the various Sons of Liberty groups that held "tea parties" in Boston, New Jersey, and elsewhere when the Tea Act was passed. The Sons of Liberty were also responsible for forming the Committees of Correspondence that kept the patriots throughout the colonies up-to-date on what was going on. It was their letters that were passed between these local committees that are credited with bringing about the First Continental Congress.

the only colony that ever issued any tax stamps was Georgia. Parliament realized that the Stamp Act was not going to work and repealed it in 1766.

## THE TOWNSHEND DUTIES AND THE TEA AND INTOLERABLE ACTS

In 1767, Parliament tried again, this time passing a series of taxes known as the Townshend Duties. These included taxes on tea, glass, paper, and lead paints. The purpose of the taxes was to pay Crown officials in the colonies. Up until this point, the governor and other royal officials in the colonies had been paid by the colonial assemblies. Townshend believed that many officials were reluctant to enforce the English laws and taxes because they depended on the goodwill of the assemblies to get paid. If they were paid directly by the Crown, there would be no question as to whose interests they served.

In 1762, William Franklin, Benjamin Franklin's son, was appointed royal governor of New Jersey. Many in the colony were pleased by his appointment. He was born in America, and many were familiar with his father's outspoken political views. However, unlike his father, Governor Franklin was a staunch Loyalist and was the royal nemesis of the people of New Jersey until independence was declared in 1776.

The protests over the Townshend Duties caused Parliament in 1770 to repeal all the taxes except the one on tea. However, it was rarely collected. The colonists in New Jersey and elsewhere had become expert at smuggling in goods that were restricted. When Parliament tried to restructure the tax on tea with the Tea Act of 1773, by lowering the price on tea while raising the tax, they thought the people of the colonies would accept it.

The Tea Act seemed to be the final blow to many in the colonies. Up until this point, no one was talking about armed rebellion. They were trying to figure out how they could get the rights they felt were due them as English subjects. In Boston, Massachusetts, on December 16, 1773, a group of patriots dumped a load of tea into Boston Harbor. In retaliation, in 1774, Parliament in London passed a series of laws, called the Coercive Acts, referred to in the colonies as the Intolerable Acts.

These acts were meant to punish the people of Boston by closing their harbor, requiring them to pay for the tea that had been destroyed, and revoking the colony's charter. For many in the

To protest the passage of the Tea Act, some male colonists, disguised as American Indians, boarded three ships in Boston Harbor on December 16, 1773, and dumped hundreds of cases of tea into the harbor. The event became known as the Boston Tea Party. *(Library of Congress)*

## New Jersey's Tea Party or the Greenwich Tea Burning

Most history books give an account of how a group of patriots disguised as Native Americans dumped a load of tea into Boston Harbor but very few give accounts of other "tea parties" elsewhere in the colonies. In December 1774, the ship the *Greyhound* sailed into Delaware Bay and unloaded a shipment of tea in Greenwich, New Jersey.

The tea was moved to the cellar of a house owned by Daniel Bowen, a Loyalist.

When local patriots found out about this, approximately 20 of them dressed up like Native Americans, broke into the house, brought the tea chests to the village green, and burned the tea. The company that owned the tea wanted to prosecute the people who had destroyed their tea. But the people of New Jersey were so upset that the case never came to trial because the belief was that no New Jersey jury would convict the men.

colonies, it was a wake-up call. They realized that they lived at the whim of the king and his councilors. Many sympathetic farmers in New Jersey sent food overland to the people of Boston. At the same time, the relationship between Governor Franklin and many in the New Jersey assembly was becoming strained.

## THE FIRST CONTINENTAL CONGRESS

As the situation between England and its colonies became more difficult, those on the side of the Patriot cause formed into loose associations known as Committees of Correspondence. These groups sent letters back and forth between the colonies and within their own colony calling for action against the Crown. It was from these Committees that the call went out for a continental congress of representatives from all the colonies to address their collective problems with England.

The First Continental Congress met in Philadelphia in September 1774. A union of the colonies was proposed at this time but was not passed. Instead, the First Continental Congress passed a nonimportation agreement that would be followed a year later by a nonexportation agreement if the grievances of the colonies had not been addressed. The Continental Congress also called upon the king to try and settle the differences between the colonies and the Crown.

The people of New Jersey were not as radical as their counterparts in Massachusetts and Virginia. Many in New Jersey, especially the Quakers in what had been West Jersey, wanted a peaceful settlement of the problems between the people of the colonies and the royal government in London.

A Provincial Congress was called by the various Committees of Correspondence in New Jersey, and they agreed to the nonimportation agreement that had passed the Continental Congress. They also agreed to send delegates to the Second Continental Congress that was to convene in Philadelphia in May 1775.

The Second Continental Congress convened on May 10, 1775, and remained in session until the newly independent nation had a constitution. *(National Archives, Still Picture Records, NWDNS-148-CCD-35)*

Events in Massachusetts once again changed the complexion of the relationship between the colonies and the Crown. On April 19, 1775, Massachusetts militia men confronted British troops in the Battles of Lexington and Concord. When English soldiers attacked colonists in Massachusetts, the debate changed.

When the Second Continental Congress went into session, they were faced with the crisis in Massachusetts. They decided to come to the aid of Boston in its struggle. George Washington was put in charge of raising 20,000 men as a continental army and liberating Boston from English occupation. The Battle of Bunker Hill was fought in Boston, and Washington was able to liberate the city on April 19, 1776. This was the last fighting that Massachusetts saw within its borders. New Jersey, which had been reluctant to enter into armed conflict with England, became one of the major battlegrounds of the War for Independence. Only South Carolina would see more battles than New Jersey.

# 6

# The War for Independence Begins

The Second Continental Congress convened in Philadelphia on May 10, 1775, and remained in session almost continuously throughout the American Revolution. New Jersey's Patriot-led Provincial Congress sent delegates to the Continental Congress and was running the colony in spite of attempts by Governor William Franklin to maintain control. On January 8, 1776, the governor and his wife were placed under house arrest by Patriots who attacked their house in Perth Amboy. The condition of the arrest was that if Franklin stayed out of politics, the Patriots representing the Provincial Congress would leave him alone.

Franklin realized that New Jersey was almost equally divided between Patriots and those loyal to England, who were called Loyalists or Tories. In June 1776, Franklin tried to reconvene the Loyalist General Assembly and was arrested by the patriot militia. Franklin was sent to Connecticut as a prisoner of war. It appeared as if New Jersey would be a stronghold for the cause of freedom. When the Declaration of Independence was passed by the Continental Congress on July 4, 1776, five representatives from New Jersey signed it. They were Richard Stockton, John Witherspoon, Francis Hopkinson, John Hart, and Abraham Clark.

Once the Continental Congress declared independence, the thirteen colonies became the "United States of America." At this point, there was no avoiding an all-out war with the British forces in North America.

# WASHINGTON'S RETREAT ACROSS NEW JERSEY

After the victories at Lexington and Concord, Bunker Hill, and the liberation of Boston, it seemed the American Revolution would be over quickly. Nothing could have been further from the truth. George Washington had moved the Continental army south to New York, where in the summer of 1776, they were repeatedly defeated by the British and forced to retreat into New Jersey.

Washington had instructed General Charles Lee to build a fort on the high ground in New Jersey that overlooked the Hudson River. The fort that was hastily constructed on the palisades was called Fort Lee. Having chased the Continental army out of New York, on November 20, 1776, a British force moved up the Hudson six miles above Fort Lee and landed on the New Jersey side of the river. Most of the Patriot forces were able to escape from Fort Lee before it was overrun by the British force, but they were forced to leave many of their supplies behind. The British under Charles, Lord Cornwallis and General William Howe chased the dwindling rebel army across New Jersey to the banks of the Delaware River.

Washington had the foresight to have all the boats on the New Jersey side of the river moved to Pennsylvania. Had he left the boats for the British, the War of Independence might have ended shortly with the British winning. As it was, Washington knew he was in trouble. As soon as the Delaware River froze solid, the British would be able to cross, and he would not stand a chance. Howe took his main force back to New York to wait for his chance to finish off Washington and his diminishing forces. Many Patriots were leaving the army as their enlistments had ended or to avoid the difficulties of spending the winter in the field.

Over the next six years, there were almost 100 battles fought in New Jersey as

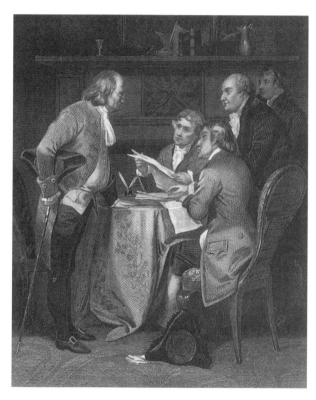

The Second Continental Congress selected a committee of five members to draft the Declaration of Independence. From left to right are Benjamin Franklin, Thomas Jefferson, Robert Livingston, John Adams, and Roger Sherman. *(Library of Congress)*

# The First Paragraph of the Declaration of Independence

*When in the Course of human events, it becomes necessary for one people to dissolve the political bands which have connected them with another, and to assume among the Powers of the earth, the separate and equal station to which the Laws of Nature and of Nature's God entitle them, a decent respect to the opinions of mankind requires that they should declare the causes which impel them to the separation.*

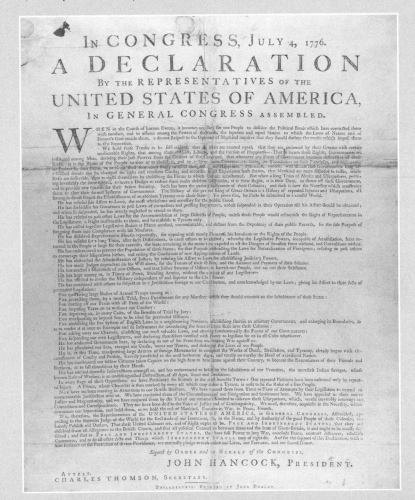

One of the first and boldest acts of the Second Continental Congress was to compose and sign the Declaration of Independence in the summer of 1776. *(National Archives, Old Military and Civil Records, NWCTB-360-ITEM1-ITEM1VOL3P94)*

When the Revolutionary War began in 1775, Charles, Lord Cornwallis volunteered to serve. This watercolor shows Cornwallis's forces landing in West New Jersey on November 20, 1776. *(National Archives, Still Picture Records, NWDNS-148-GW-365)*

## General William Howe, Fifth Viscount Howe
### (1729–1814)

General William Howe was second in command to General Thomas Gage in Boston in 1775. Later that year, he took over as commander of the British forces in North America. He has often been criticized for not pursuing the Americans vigorously enough. But others have argued that there were a number of extenuating circumstances that forced him to pursue the rebels in a conservative fashion. First, he had to depend on getting supplies from England, and American privateers were disrupting his supply lines. Another consideration was he had no reinforcements. If a soldier was killed, captured, or knocked out of action by wounds, Howe was not able to replace him.

In 1778, when he did not follow Washington to Valley Forge and finally defeat him, Howe received so much criticism that he resigned and returned to England. The reason he gave for his resignation was lack of support for the war from England.

the Americans headquartered in Philadelphia and the British based in New York fought over the ground in between. In the course of the war, more than 17,000 New Jerseyans fought in the war either as members of the Continental army or in the New Jersey militia. Their first victory came at Trenton, and it gave hope to the desperate forces of freedom.

## THE BATTLES OF TRENTON AND PRINCETON

George Washington and what he had left for an army were in a tough spot. If they did nothing, it would only be a matter of time before Cornwallis and Howe brought the fight to them. Throughout the war, Washington employed the techniques he had learned in the French and Indian Wars on how to fight a larger and better-trained conventional army. The European armies of the time would line up opposite each other on a battlefield and exchange cannon and rifle fire until one side was forced to retreat. In such a battle, the outnumbered and ill-equipped American forces would have been overwhelmed.

The Continental army at its largest point had only 20,000 members. Between the British and their paid mercenaries, the Hessians, there were between 40,000 and 50,000 troops available to fight the rebels. Washington preferred to use sneak attacks against equal or weaker forces where he could gain an objective and then retreat if necessary.

Once he had crossed the Delaware River, Washington decided it was time to go back and surprise the garrisons that General Howe had left in New Jersey to protect the interests of New Jersey Loyalists. The first focus of his plan was to capture a Hessian force

### Hessians

To ensure they had sufficient troops to fight the American rebels, the British hired German mercenaries called Hessians. These were professional soldiers who were used in a variety of ways by the British. In New Jersey, they were given the task of holding a number of towns.

at Trenton. The plan called for his men to sneak back across the river on Christmas night, December 25, 1776.

This was a bold plan that might not have succeeded if Washington had not had a group of troops from Marblehead, Massachusetts, who were experienced fishermen who could handle the boats. In the dark of night, with snow and rain spitting from the sky and large chunks of ice flowing in the swollen river, the Marblehead volunteers rowed their commandeered flat-bottomed boats back and forth across the Delaware.

Back in New Jersey, Washington split his force so that Trenton and the Hessians would be attacked from the north and the south at the same time. The American soldiers had all been issued a blanket before they crossed the river. The blankets gave them some protection from the snow and freezing rain, but more important, they

On December 25, 1776, George Washington and his troops crossed the Delaware River in a sneak attack on the Hessians, German mercenaries hired by the British, at Trenton. *(National Archives, Still Pictures Branch, NWDNS-66-G-15D[25])*

George Washington and his troops surprised the British and Hessians at Trenton by attacking them the morning after Christmas Day. *(National Archives/DOD, War & Conflict, #30)*

were able to keep their flintlocks dry so their rifles would still fire when they reached Trenton.

Due to the storm and Christmas celebrations, the Hessians had cut back on their patrols that night, and the two forces arrived at Trenton undetected. At 8 A.M. on December 26, 1776, General Stephen's forces attacked and overwhelmed a Hessian outpost. Three minutes later, General Sullivan's soldiers attacked from the other side of town.

The surprised Hessians were soon overrun by the rebel forces. About 500 Hessians escaped, and the rest of the regiment was captured. Washington returned to Pennsylvania with his captives. He sent them to Philadelphia, where they were paraded through the streets to bolster the sagging hopes of the people there. At this point, it is speculated that Washington had learned a valuable lesson

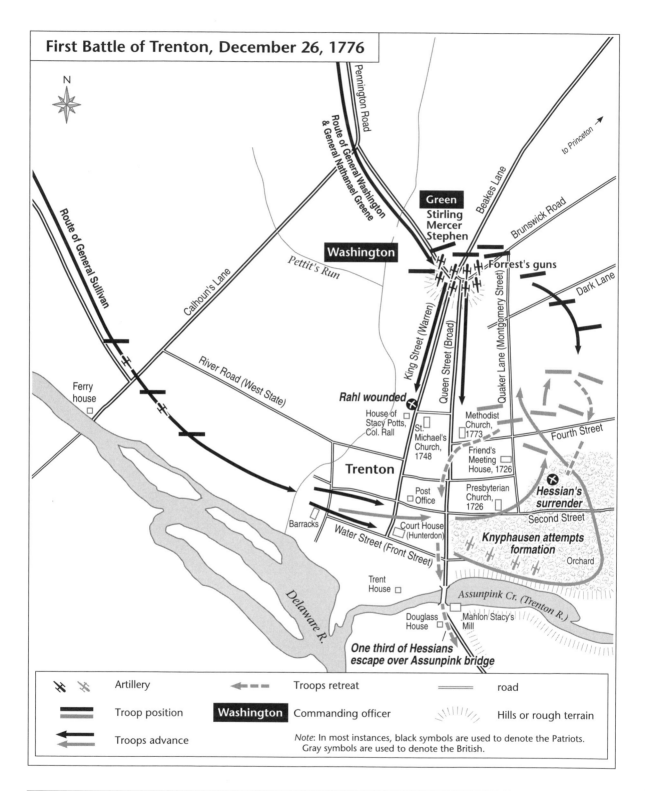

# First Battle of Trenton, December 26, 1776

N

Pennington Road

Route of General Washington & General Nathanael Greene

to Princeton

Beakes Lane

Brunswick Road

**Green**
Stirling
Mercer
Stephen

**Washington**

**Forrest's guns**

Dark Lane

Route of General Sullivan

Calhoun's Lane

*Pettit's Run*

King Street (Warren)

Queen Street (Broad)

Quaker Lane (Montgomery Street)

River Road (West State)

Ferry house

*Rahl wounded*

House of Stacy Potts, Col. Rall

St. Michael's Church, 1748

Methodist Church, 1773

Fourth Street

Friend's Meeting House, 1726

**Hessian's surrender**

**Trenton**

Post Office

Presbyterian Church, 1726

Second Street

**Knyphausen attempts formation**

Barracks

Water Street (Front Street)

Court House (Hunterdon)

Orchard

Trent House

*Assunpink Cr. (Trenton R.)*

Delaware R.

Douglass House

Mahlon Stacy's Mill

*One third of Hessians escape over Assunpink bridge*

| | | |
|---|---|---|
| ⚔ ⚔ Artillery | ◀--- Troops retreat | road |
| — Troop position | **Washington** Commanding officer | Hills or rough terrain |
| ◀ Troops advance | | |

*Note*: In most instances, black symbols are used to denote the Patriots. Gray symbols are used to denote the British.

As this painting by John Trumbull shows, George Washington captured many of the Hessians at Trenton. Many other Hessians escaped, however. *(Library of Congress, Prints and Photographs Division [LC-D416-699])*

as to how to fight the British forces, and he took his men back across the Delaware to Trenton on December 30, 1776.

In the meantime, Lord Cornwallis had set out from New York with a force of 5,500 soldiers. As Cornwallis approached Trenton late in the day on January 1, 1777, he thought he had Washington trapped. There had been a number of bloody skirmishes that had delayed the advance of the British. When they tried to cross the bridge over Assunpink Creek, the British were repelled three times

*Opposite page:* Early in the morning of December 26, 1776, George Washington slipped back into New Jersey and captured a regiment of Hessians that were garrisoned at Trenton, New Jersey.

*Opposite page:* When Lord Cornwallis thought he had George Washington's army pinned down at the Second Battle of Trenton, Washington slipped away in the night and won a victory at Princeton.

before Cornwallis decided to wait until morning and organize his final attack on the Americans.

Realizing the precariousness of his position, Washington had his men sneak away in the night. He left behind only enough troops to keep the campfires burning and a few to dig trenches so Cornwallis would think the entire American force was still there. With Cornwallis in Trenton, Washington planned another sneak attack, this time on Princeton, New Jersey.

George Washington and troops defeated the British at the Battle of Princeton on January 3, 1777, the end of the "10 crucial days" of fighting that helped boost the Patriots' morale. *(National Archives/DOD, War & Conflict, #32)*

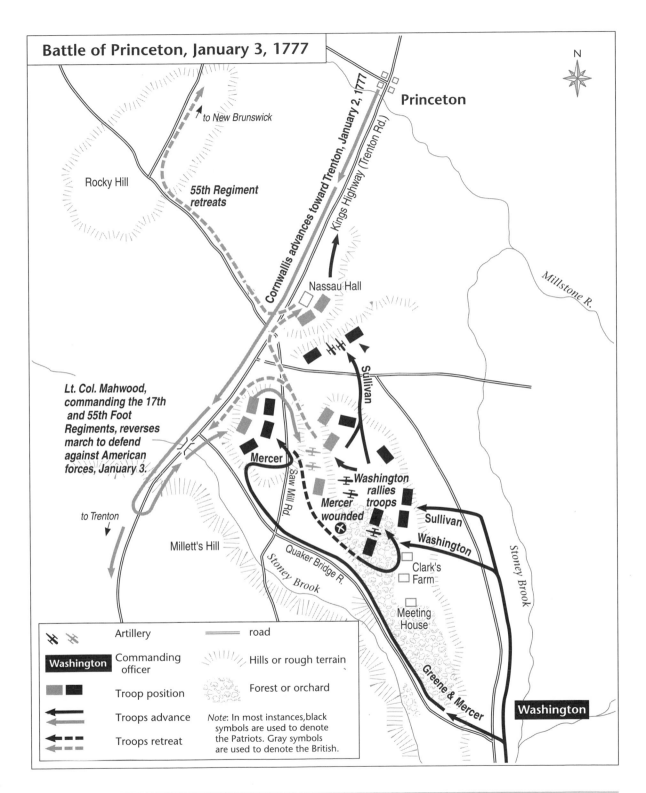

# Battle of Princeton, January 3, 1777

N

Princeton

to New Brunswick

Cornwallis advances toward Trenton, January 2, 1777

Kings Highway (Trenton Rd.)

Rocky Hill

**55th Regiment retreats**

Nassau Hall

Millstone R.

Sullivan

*Lt. Col. Mahwood, commanding the 17th and 55th Foot Regiments, reverses march to defend against American forces, January 3.*

**Mercer**

**Washington rallies troops**

**Mercer wounded**

**Sullivan**

**Washington**

to Trenton

Millett's Hill

Saw Mill Rd.

Quaker Bridge R.

Stoney Brook

Clark's Farm

Meeting House

Stoney Brook

Greene & Mercer

**Washington**

| Symbol | Meaning | Symbol | Meaning |
|---|---|---|---|
| Artillery | | road | |
| Washington | Commanding officer | Hills or rough terrain | |
| Troop position | | Forest or orchard | |
| Troops advance | | | |
| Troops retreat | | | |

*Note*: In most instances, black symbols are used to denote the Patriots. Gray symbols are used to denote the British.

## Princeton University

In 1746, the legislature of New Jersey granted a charter to the College of New Jersey and it became the fourth college in North America. The first year it was open, the college held classes in Elizabeth. It then moved to Newark in 1747 and then to Princeton in 1756. Despite the fact that the Revolutionary War raged through New Jersey, classes continued. In 1896, it changed its name to Princeton University.

This 1895 photograph shows a bird's-eye view of Princeton University. *(Library of Congress, Prints and Photographs Division [LC-USZ62-125529])*

When the American forces reached Princeton on January 3, 1777, they were met by strong resistance. When part of his troops were attacked by the British, it looked like Washington's plan would end in disaster, but he personally took to the battlefield and rallied his troops. When Cornwallis realized that Washington had slipped away from the trap in Trenton, he headed for Princeton. The Americans had won the battle, and left before Cornwallis could get there.

Washington then moved his army northward to Morristown, where they spent the rest of the winter. Cornwallis decided to retire from the field and abandoned most of New Jersey for the rest of the winter. Although none of these battles are considered major military victories, the time between December 25, 1776, and January 3, 1777, is often referred to as the "ten crucial days." The success of the American forces gave hope to the patriot cause. It would take four years to bring the American Revolution to a final victory.

Without the battles of Trenton and Princeton, it might have ended much sooner with a different outcome.

## WAR-TORN NEW JERSEY

The winter in Morristown was extremely difficult for the American troops. Many of the soldiers were forced to live in small huts. There were constant shortages of food and other supplies. In addition, many soldiers had signed up for relatively short enlistments in the army and went home. Others deserted rather than suffer the harsh conditions. By spring, Washington had only 4,000 troops at Morristown. It was uncertain how many new recruits would arrive before the fighting began.

Although no major battles were fought in New Jersey in 1777, sporadic fighting was almost constant as small groups of British and American forces clashed while patrolling New Jersey

George Washington and his troops spent the winter of 1777–78 at Valley Forge, Pennsylvania, about 20 miles from Philadelphia, occupied at that time by the British. The colonial forces had little food or supplies at their winter camp. *(National Archives/DOD, War & Conflict, #35)*

between Philadelphia and New York. It was a time of near anarchy in New Jersey.

There were constant conflicts between Loyalists and patriots. While the major conflict moved south and west as the American forces unsuccessfully tried to defend Philadelphia, armed bands of Loyalists fought a guerilla campaign against the patriots of New Jersey. Groups of Patriots did the same as they confiscated Loyalist property and retaliated against their Loyalist neighbors. Houses and barns were burned, crops were destroyed, and people were in constant fear for their safety. Atrocities were committed by both sides as New Jersey remained in a near state of civil war throughout the Revolution.

Along the coast, privateers attacked British shipping that was trying to keep the British supplied. The struggling navy that the

Continental Congress had authorized was no match for the huge fleet of British warships. However, more than 2,400 privateers throughout the states were commissioned to attack British shipping. During the war, both Little Egg Harbor and Toms River were attacked by the British from the sea in an attempt to stop the privateers.

The farmers of New Jersey also played a role in the war. Patriot farmers profited by selling food and grain to Washington's army. Loyalists who still had their farms sold their goods to the British in New York. It is reported that some enterprising farmers sold their produce to both sides.

Rather than run the gauntlet of Washington's forces in New Jersey, Cornwallis led a campaign to capture Philadelphia by sailing up the Chesapeake Bay. After defeating the Americans at the Battles of Brandywine and Germantown, Cornwallis marched into Philadelphia. Washington and his army were forced to spend a very difficult winter in the snow and cold at Valley Forge, Pennsylvania.

# 7

# The Tide Turns in the War for Independence

After the terrible winter at Valley Forge, spring 1778 found Washington once again in New Jersey. Now he was between two British forces—one in Philadelphia and the other in New York. When Sir Henry Clinton marched out of Philadelphia in June 1778, Washington once again crossed the Delaware planning to harass and eventually attack Clinton. There was a difference in the army that took the field in 1778. Over the winter, a Prussian baron had arrived in North America and volunteered to help the struggling Continental army. Baron von Steuben was appointed inspector general of the army. He reorganized Washington's forces, prepared a manual of tactics, and drilled the men into a more efficient fighting force that was able to hold its own in a pitched battle with the British troops.

Another volunteer in the American army, the marquis de Lafayette from France was sent out to attack the supply wagons and rearguard of the Clinton force, which was soon stretched out over a great distance. Clinton halted his march at Monmouth Court House to give his supplies a chance to catch up with his main force. It was here that Washington attacked.

The battle plan called for General Lee to attack at dawn on June 28, 1778, with a small force. For reasons that were never explained, he waited until after 8:00 A.M. to engage the enemy. Shortly thereafter, he ordered his men to retreat. When Washington came up with the main force of his army, he was extremely

## The Marquis de Lafayette
### (1757–1834)

The ideas of the American Revolution caught the imagination of many in Europe. Marie Joseph Paul Yves Roch Gilbert du Motier, marquis de Lafayette, was one of them. He came to North America in 1777 and was granted a special commission in the Continental army by the Congress. He had been a captain in the French army and was given the rank of major general by the Americans. He became a member of Washington's staff and was one of the general's closest confidants. He was wounded at the Battle of the Brandywine and was division commander at the Battle of Monmouth.

When France made an alliance with the United States against the British, Lafayette returned to France and lobbied on behalf of France's new allies. He is credited with convincing the French to supply military and financial aid to the Americans. In 1780, he returned to North America and fought with distinction in the Virginia campaign that brought the war to an end with the surrender of Cornwallis at the Battle of Yorktown in 1781. At the end of the war, Lafayette returned to France, where he was a moderate voice for freedom and reform in French politics.

In 1784, he returned to the United States and was given a hero's welcome. He was later voted a gift of $200,000 and a large section of land by Congress. In 1917, during World War I, when the American Expeditionary Forces arrived in France to join the war against Germany, General Pershing called upon his aide Colonel Charles E. Stanton to give a speech at Lafayette's tomb. Stanton stepped up to the podium and expressed the feelings of many American soldiers simply and eloquently when he said, "Lafayette, we are here."

upset. He berated Lee for not following orders and for quitting the battle without cause. Lee was relieved of his command and Washington personally rallied the troops, and the Battle of Monmouth continued.

As the day wore on, the temperature rose to over 100° Fahrenheit. Both people and horses succumbed to the heat. At the end of the day, the battle had been fought to a draw and Clinton was able to get most of his force to the safety of New York. Washington felt that after fighting all day in the heat, his men needed rest more than they needed to catch the retreating Clinton.

There were many instances of heroism during the Revolution. One of the most famous took place at the Battle of Monmouth. Often the wives of soldiers followed their husbands. Most of the time, they would stay safely in the background away from the fighting. Sometimes they would bring food and water to the soldiers during a battle. At the Battle of Monmouth, a young woman, Mary Ludwig Hays, who became known as "Molly Pitcher," went one step further when her husband, who was an artillery officer, went down. She stepped in and took his place, helping to keep his cannon firing throughout the battle.

After the Battle of Monmouth, Washington's army spent the rest of the summer and early fall of 1778 keeping the British

On July 28, 1778, after surviving a fierce winter at Valley Forge, George Washington and his troops nearly defeated the British at the Battle of Monmouth. *(National Archives, Still Picture Records, NWDNS-148-GW-95)*

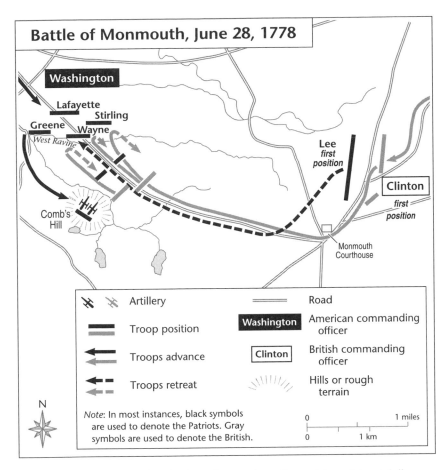

## Battle of Monmouth, June 28, 1778

**Washington**

Lafayette
Stirling
Greene
Wayne
*West Ravine*

Comb's
Hill

Lee
*first
position*

**Clinton**
*first
position*

Monmouth
Courthouse

| | | |
|---|---|---|
| ✳ ✳ | Artillery | ════ Road |
| ▬ ▬ | Troop position | **Washington** American commanding officer |
| ◀━ ◀━ | Troops advance | Clinton British commanding officer |
| ◀- ◀- | Troops retreat | ⁄⁄⁄⁄⁄ Hills or rough terrain |

*Note*: In most instances, black symbols are used to denote the Patriots. Gray symbols are used to denote the British.

N

0                1 miles
0        1 km

Despite early confusion by the Americans when General Lee did not follow the battle plan, Washington was able to rally the rebel forces and fight British General Clinton to a draw.

forces contained in New York. In November, Washington moved his forces to Middlebrook, where they had the time to build a proper winter camp. Winter 1778–79 turned out to be extremely mild, and the American army got through it with relative ease. It made a pleasant comparison to the two previous winters spent in Valley Forge, Pennsylvania, and Morristown, New Jersey.

During 1779, the war remained a stalemate in the North, with the British forces fortified in New York and Washington's army

# Molly Pitcher
## (1753–1832)

Mary Ludwig Hays followed her husband to war as he served as an artillery officer in the Pennsylvania State Regiment of Artillery. During the extreme heat of the Battle of Monmouth, she helped out by bringing pitchers of water to the men at their battle stations. Her husband called her Molly, and his men quickly nicknamed her "Molly Pitcher" for the job she was doing. It is reported that her husband was either wounded, or, like many that day, succumbed to the heat. When he was no longer able to help his men, Molly jumped in and took his place. She was one of only a handful of women who saw action in the Revolution.

Called "Molly" by her husband, Mary Ludwig Hays brought pitchers of water to the colonial troops during the June 1778 Battle of Monmouth, for which she was nicknamed "Molly Pitcher." When her husband was injured (or succumbed to the terribly hot weather) during the fighting, she took his place working with the artillery. *(National Archives/DOD, War & Conflict, #37)*

At the end of the Battle of Monmouth, General Washington personally thanked her for her heroic deed. He made her a sergeant in the army, and she was referred to as "Sergeant Molly." After the war, she returned to Pennsylvania and was later granted a soldier's pension by the Pennsylvania legislature. A cannon stands at her gravesite in Carlisle, Pennsylvania, and her heroic deed is depicted on the battle monument at Monmouth.

containing them. Washington returned to Morristown to spend the winter of 1779–80. It turned out to be one of the worst winters on record. Numerous snowstorms piled up deep snow and made it extremely hard to keep the army supplied.

In the spring, a number of small battles were fought in New Jersey at Springfield and Elizabethtown and at Camden. However, the main focus of the war had turned to the South. The War of Independence came to an end when Lord Cornwallis surrendered to

After seven years of fighting, General Cornwallis surrendered at Yorktown on October 17, 1781. *(National Archives)*

The British and the newly independent United States finally compromised when they signed the Treaty of Paris in 1783, two years after the fighting had stopped in the colonies. *(Library of Congress, Prints and Photographs Division [LC-USZ6-279])*

George Washington on October 19, 1781, at the Siege of Yorktown. However, it took almost two years for the two sides to agree on the terms of the Treaty of Paris in 1783. For the people of New Jersey, the end of the war meant it was time to try and rebuild their state.

# 8

# The State of New Jersey

## NEW JERSEY GETS A CONSTITUTION

The transition from royal colony to state was a difficult one for most of the thirteen colonies. This held true in New Jersey, especially in the first years of independence. As the Second Continental Congress hammered out the Declaration of Independence in 1776, a number of colonies were planning their own independence by writing and adopting new constitutions.

New Jersey was among these. The Reverend Jacob Green and others wrote a number of articles calling for independence from Britain. When the Congress suggested that the states adopt their own constitutions, New Jersey's Provincial Congress voted 54-3 to adopt a new constitution. On June 24, 1776, Green was selected chairman of the committee that wrote New Jersey's first constitution.

The document they came up with was not really a radical change. For the most part, it borrowed from the colony's royal charter with a few major changes. Probably because of the state's terrible experiences with royal governors like Cornbury and Andros, the New Jersey constitution gave the assembly most of the power to make laws and run the government. The governor had very few powers. The New Jersey state constitution was adopted by an overwhelming majority on July 2, 1776.

The first governor of New Jersey under its new constitution was William Livingston. Despite his lack of powers under the new

William Livingston served as the first governor of New Jersey after the state constitution was adopted July 2, 1776. *(New Jersey Historical Society)*

constitution, Livingston proved to be an able leader and was governor from 1776 until his death in 1790. As governor during the Revolution, Livingston was declared an outlaw by the British in New York and a £2,000 reward was placed on his head. There were reportedly many attempts to kill or kidnap him. For one stretch during the war, Livingston never slept in the same place for more than two days in a row and had to be constantly on guard.

One other interesting aspect of the New Jersey state constitution was its expansion of voting rights. The document called for reducing the property requirements to vote so that all adult males would be given the right to vote. The language of the voting requirements, which referred to "freeholders" and "all inhabitants," created a loophole that gave the women of New Jersey the right to vote, which they did starting in 1790. Women continued voting in New Jersey until November 16, 1807, when the legislature changed the law. Some have said that this language was intentionally placed in the state constitution by Joseph Cooper, a Quaker from West Jersey.

During the war, Livingston spent most of his energy trying to aid New Jersey's units in the Continental army as well as its militia. With Washington and his army spending a number of years fighting in and around New Jersey, it was a monumental task. The new state government amassed a sizable debt during the war that was just one of many problems it faced when the war ended.

## WINNING THE PEACE

In 1781, the people of New Jersey watched as General Washington and the Continental army and a French army led by the comte de Rochambeau marched southward through the state, to the final showdown with Lord Cornwallis at Yorktown, Virginia. The state they left behind was in a state of near ruin.

# William Livingston
## (1723–1790)

William Livingston came from an influential family and was born in Albany, New York. When he was 14, his family sent him to spend a year with an English missionary who lived with the Mohawk, a group of Native Americans in upstate New York. It was felt that the experience in the wilderness among Native Americans would be of value if William Livingston went into the family fur business.

Instead of going into the fur business, Livingston went to Yale College in Connecticut and then became a lawyer in New York City. In 1745, Livingston married Susanna French, whose family were wealthy landowners in New Jersey. The Livingstons had 13 children. Livingston became a very successful lawyer in New York and nearby New Jersey.

When the political party he belonged to in New York fell out of power, Livingston bought land near Elizabeth, New Jersey. He built a large home that he named Liberty Hall and spent his days as a gentleman farmer, raising his large family. When the War for Independence started, he joined the cause and soon became governor in 1776.

In addition to being New Jersey's governor for 14 years, he was a delegate to both the First and Second Continental Congresses and the Constitutional Convention. After the Revolution, Livingston showed he was an advocate for freedom for all people when he freed the two slaves he owned and became an active abolitionist.

A law passed in 1777 had allowed the state to confiscate hundreds of properties that belonged to Loyalists. Many of the Loyalists were forced into exile to Nova Scotia, Canada. Governor Franklin, who had been arrested and imprisoned in Connecticut, was released in a prisoner exchange and lived the rest of his life in England on a pension granted him by the king. There were other Loyalists who managed to hold on to their lands, and areas such as the strongly Dutch Bergen County continued to elect Tories to the state legislature into the 1780s.

One of the biggest problems facing New Jersey was the damage caused by the more than 100 battles that had been fought there. In the towns that stretched out along the routes between Philadelphia and New York, there was hardly a school or church

Depicted in this painting by Charles Wilson Peale, Jean-Baptiste-Donatien de Vimeur, comte de Rochambeau, commanded the French army during the Revolutionary War. *(Library of Congress, Prints and Photographs Division [LC-USZ62-121988])*

building that had not been seriously damaged. Many were totally destroyed by one side or the other. In Middlesex County, which is located in the northeastern part of the state around Perth Amboy, more than 650 private properties were damaged by the war.

The anarchy of the war years had left schools closed. Libraries and other public buildings had been plundered. In the freewheeling time of war, many in New Jersey had profited by supplying the British, the Americans, or both. With the end of the war, the markets for their farm produce and other goods dried up. As the markets vanished, the supply of money in the colony also decreased.

There were also serious problems with war debts, both at the state and federal level. In June 1783, angry former soldiers, who had yet to be paid for their service in the Continental army, marched on the U.S. capital in Philadelphia. Rather than confront these disgruntled veterans of the Revolution, the members of Congress slipped across the Delaware River and reconvened at Princeton, New Jersey, which briefly housed the capital of the new United States. Nassau Hall at the College of New Jersey (now called Princeton University) served as the national capitol from June 30 to November 4, 1783. The Congress returned to New Jersey one other time during the years before the national capitol was built on the banks of the Potomac River. Trenton hosted the Congress from November 1 to December 24, 1784.

It was under the guidance of Livingston and the leaders of the state legislature that New Jersey worked its way through this difficult time. The legislature seemed to divide once again between East and West Jersey. The farmers who owned small farms in the East wanted the state to issue paper money that

Trenton, the current capital of New Jersey, hosted the country's congress briefly in 1784. The building in this illustration is the state capitol building, which was built in 1794. *(Library of Congress, Prints and Photographs Division [LC-USZ62-94851])*

would make it easier for them to pay their debts. The large land owners and more wealthy representatives from the West wanted the money supply to remain tight so they would not be paid off by debtors with devalued currency.

The question of currency may not seem very important in these days of a solid dollar and adequate money supply, but in post-revolutionary New Jersey it was critical. At one point in 1786, thousands of people petitioned the state to issue more paper money. At the same time, there were those with strong objections to the issuance of paper money because they feared the devaluation of their assets.

New Jersey steered a steady and moderate course through these difficult times, with the governor and the legislature finding the

# Soft versus Hard Money

One of the problems that faced the American colonies almost from the beginning was a lack of currency. Hard money, in the form of gold and silver coins, was scarce and acquired primarily through trade with the Caribbean. The Spanish silver dollar was the most common coin in the colonies. It was often cut into eight pieces that were called bits. Two bits would equal a quarter of a dollar, four bits would be a half dollar, and eight bits would equal one dollar. The term *two bits* is still sometimes heard when someone is referring to a quarter. Due to the lack of coins, many states allowed wampum to be used as currency.

In addition to hard money, a number of colonies issued varying amounts of paper money. Paper money was considered soft money, as it had no real value. It created many problems. It was subject to wide swings in value, and there was no standardization between the states. During the Revolution, the Continental Congress issued paper money that became almost worthless. However, many people favored paper money because it made it easier for them to pay their debts and taxes. The financial crisis that faced many of the colonies under the Articles of Confederation was a major factor in the creation of a stronger federal government under the Constitution of 1787.

These paper bills were issued by the Continental Congress during the Revolutionary War. *(from Benson Lossing,* The Pictorial Field-Book of the Revolution, *1851–1852)*

## Articles of Confederation

The first draft of the Articles of Confederation that was presented to the Second Continental Congress in 1776 called for a strong central government, equal representation by the 13 states, federal control over western lands, and the power to levy taxes. To many of the more radical members of Congress, it sounded like they would just be swapping one despotic ruler for another. Congress revised the articles, returning most of the power to the states. Even after the articles were changed, many were reluctant to establish a central government. There were many differences between the colonies, as well as disagreements between them. Boundary lines between the colonies were often unclear, and there were a number of disagreements over claims to lands west of the Appalachian Mountains. Also, laws and tariffs varied from state to state.

The Articles of Confederation were not ratified until the war was almost over in 1781. Almost immediately, people realized that the government created was almost completely ineffectual. Some may have liked the lack of an effective federal government, but most came to realize that changes to the articles would have to be made. At the time, few foresaw the Constitution that would replace it.

middle road on many issues. On one issue, though, the weakness of the Articles of Confederation, New Jersey was in the vanguard in calling for a stronger central government. The United States under the Articles of Confederation, adopted in 1780, made for a weak central government that had no way of raising money to operate. It was forced to ask the states for financial support. Under the articles, the federal government usually received about 10 percent of the dollars they asked for.

Under the articles, states were given the power to collect tariffs on goods that passed through its state's ports. New Jersey at first tried to attract business by not charging any tariffs. New Jersey's free-trade position angered its bigger neighbors, New York and Pennsylvania. However, New Jersey merchants did not have the capital to compete with the markets of New York and Philadelphia.

Therefore, most of the goods imported into New Jersey ended up putting money into the pockets of the state treasuries of its

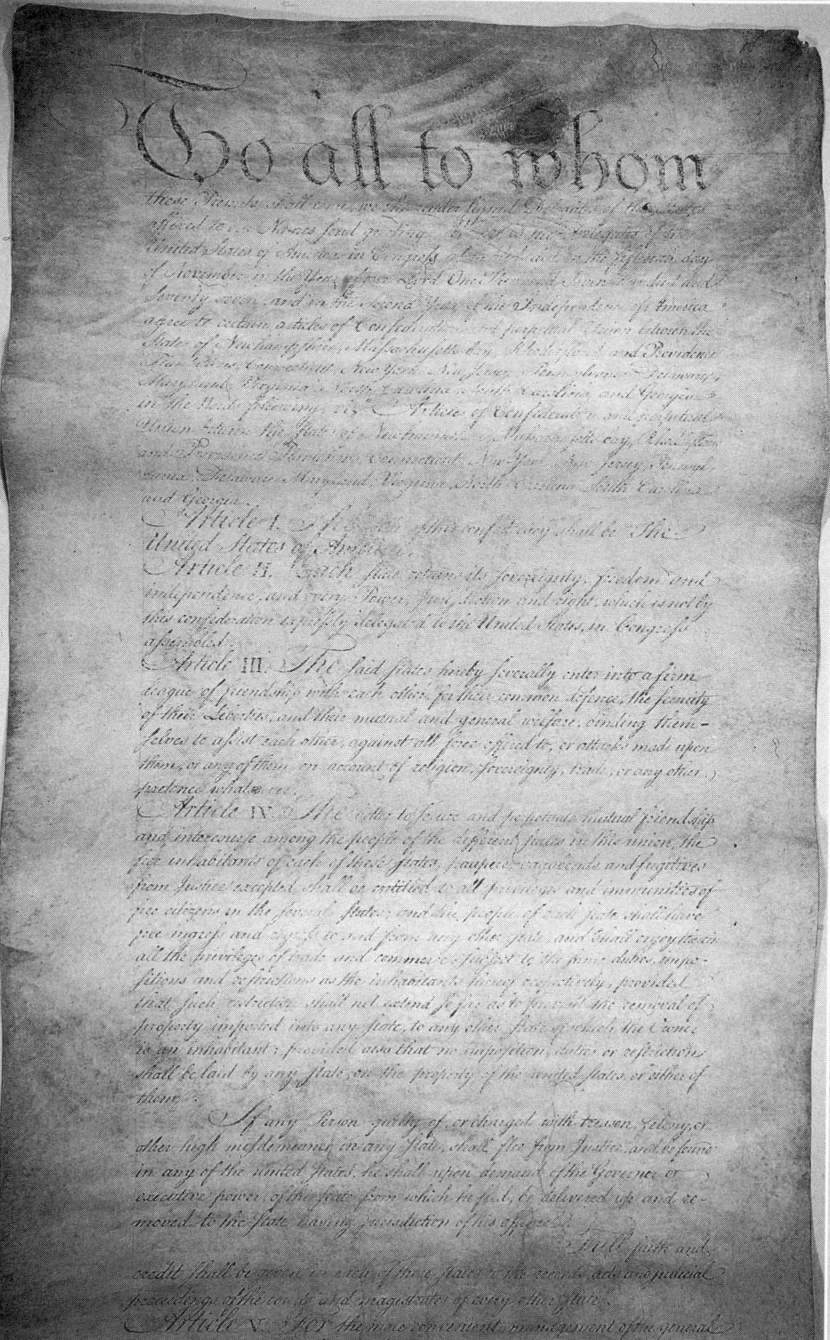

neighbors. New Jersey wanted the federal government to take over the levying and collecting of tariffs. The revolutionary slogan of "taxation without representation" was heard once again in New Jersey. In an effort to bring the situation to a crisis, in 1783, New Jersey's legislature voted to withhold any contributions to the federal government.

Another issue that upset the people of New Jersey was the lands west of the Appalachian Mountains. States such as New York, Pennsylvania, and Virginia, based on their original charters, claimed large tracts of land to the west. New Jersey and some of the other states without western land claims felt that this land should be ceded to the federal government. This would allow the federal government a source of income as the lands were developed and would help even the playing field between the states.

When New Jersey again refused to send any funds to the federal government in 1786, Congress sent a three-man delegation to the New Jersey legislature in an unsuccessful attempt to get them to change their minds. New Jersey's refusal to support the federal government under the Articles of Confederation was one of the major factors that brought about the Constitutional Convention in 1787.

*Opposite page:* The Articles of Confederation, shown here, were written by a committee of the Continental Congress and intended as a constitution for the colonies. *(National Archives, National Archives Building, NWCTB-360-MISC-ROLL10F81)*

# 9

# Building a Nation

## GETTING TO THE CONSTITUTIONAL CONVENTION

Under the limited powers of the Articles of Confederation adopted by Congress in 1780, the individual states were as likely to go their own ways as they were to come together as one strong nation. The federal government had yet to settle on a permanent capital. Many in New Jersey understood this and saw the need for the national government to have its own sources of revenue. The most obvious way to do this was to give the federal government the power to regulate trade and impose tariffs.

People in other states held the same beliefs, and a meeting of the states was called for September 11, 1786, at Annapolis, Maryland. This meeting is known as the

Abraham Clark represented New Jersey at the Second Continental Congress, where he signed the Declaration of Independence, and at the Annapolis Convention, precursor to the Constitutional Convention, to which only five states sent delegates. *(New Jersey Historical Society)*

# The Bid for the National Capital

One of the issues that faced the United States after the Revolution was where to have the national capital. The First and Second Continental Congresses had met in Philadelphia, which the Congress left in 1783 when confronted by a mob of veterans seeking their back pay. The Congress reconvened at Nassau Hall in Princeton, New Jersey, where it finished its session in 1783.

It was decided at that time that the national capital would rotate between Annapolis, Maryland, and Trenton, New Jersey. The government met in both places, but a permanent home for the capital was still a point of negotiation. The legislature of New Jersey offered Congress 20 square miles of land near the falls of the Delaware and £30,000 for building the capital in New Jersey.

*(continues)*

Nassau Hall at the College of New Jersey, now Princeton University, was the national capital for about four months in 1783. *(Library of Congress, Prints and Photographs Division [HABS, NJ, 11-PRINT, 4B-1])*

*(continued)*

Trenton turned out to be too small a town for the national capital, as the state legislature was meeting there at the same time. At that point, New York became the temporary capital. However, the people of New Jersey were still hopeful, and the second offer from the legislature offered land and $100,000.

Behind the scenes, other negotiations were going on. Alexander Hamilton needed the southern states to back his plan to have the federal government assume the debts that the states had incurred during the war. For their support, Hamilton agreed to see to it that the national capital would be built on the Potomac River in Virginia. Hamilton's deal was made and Washington, D.C., became the national capital.

Annapolis Convention. All the states were asked to send delegates who were empowered to discuss the regulation of commerce. The legislature of New Jersey thought this was a good idea and immediately selected three delegates to attend. New Jersey went one step further in that it authorized its delegates—Abraham Clark, William Churchill Houston, and James Schureman—to bring up "other important Matters."

The Annapolis Convention was unable to make much progress toward its stated goals. Only five states—Delaware, New Jersey, New York, Pennsylvania, and Virginia—sent delegates. What did come out of the Annapolis Convention was a report that called for a national convention to discuss the "important defects in the system of the Federal Government." The report also suggested that the delegates to the convention be given wide powers like those granted to the New Jersey delegates at Annapolis. It also asked that the convention "meet at Philadelphia on the second Monday in May next [1787]."

Between the time the call went out for the Annapolis Convention and the convening of the Constitutional Convention in 1787, many people had changed their minds about strengthening the federal government. A group of farmers in western Massachusetts, who were in serious financial difficulties and in danger of losing their farms, rebelled. This incident is known as Shays's Rebellion after Daniel Shays, one of its leaders. The citizens of other states were also experiencing financial problems that were complicated by the weakness of the federal government.

Where as only five states sent representatives to the Annapolis Convention, 12 states sent delegates to Philadelphia in May 1787. Rhode Island was the only state that did not have representatives at the Constitutional Convention. The delegates were charged with the task of revising the Articles of Confederation.

## NEW JERSEY AND THE CONSTITUTIONAL CONVENTION

As soon as word went out that there would be a constitutional convention, New Jersey named delegates. Governor William Livingston led the New Jersey delegates to Philadelphia. The legislature also selected David Brearley, Jonathan Dayton, William Churchill Houston, and William Paterson. All five had been active during the Revolution and hoped to preserve the union.

Jonathan Dayton represented New Jersey at the Constitutional Convention, where he helped write and signed the Constitution of the United States. *(New Jersey Historical Society)*

When the delegates convened, their first act was to expand their job. It was decided that the convention would write a completely new constitution. One of the most difficult questions that faced the delegates was how the states would be represented in the federal legislature. The large states wanted to follow what was known as the Virginia Plan. This would give states representation based entirely on their population.

William Paterson of New Jersey became one of the leaders of the convention. He put forth an alternative to the Virginia Plan. Paterson's plan became known as the New Jersey Plan. The New Jersey Plan was favored by the smaller states and suggested that each state, regardless of its size or population, should have the same number of representatives in the Congress.

A leader at the Constitutional Convention, William Paterson also served as a U.S. senator from New Jersey and was later appointed as a justice to the Supreme Court. *(New Jersey Historical Society)*

The convention almost came to an impasse over the two conflicting plans. However, a solution was found in what is known as the "Great Compromise." What was finally agreed upon was a combination of the Virginia and New Jersey Plans. The Constitution called for the federal legislature that still exists today. The Senate includes two representatives from each state, while each state is allotted seats in the House of Representatives based on population. This is known as a bicameral form of government and has turned out to be one of the great strengths of the U.S. government.

By September 1787, the new Constitution passed the Convention by unanimous consent. On September 17, 1787, it was signed by all but three of the delegates present. William Churchill Houston had been forced to leave the Convention because of illness, but the other four New Jersey delegates— William Livingston, William Paterson, David Brearley, and Jonathan Dayton—signed the new constitution.

## RATIFYING THE CONSTITUTION

The new Constitution required nine states to ratify it before it would replace the Articles of Confederation. Livingston, Paterson, and the other New Jersey delegates were pleased with the document and pushed for its ratification. When the New Jersey legislature convened in October 1787, they acted quickly to set up a convention to ratify the Constitution.

An election was held in November, and each county elected three delegates to the state convention. The convention convened at the Blazing Star Tavern in Trenton on December 11, 1787. John Stevens was elected president of the convention. Stevens had served in a variety of political positions in New Jersey since 1751, when he was first elected to the General Assembly. He was also one of the wealthiest people in the state.

## William Paterson
### (1745–1806)

William Paterson came to New Jersey from Ireland with his family when he was just two years old. His family settled near Princeton, New Jersey, and prospered as storekeepers and landowners. His family was wealthy enough to send Paterson to the College of New Jersey (Princeton), from which he graduated in 1763. After college, Paterson studied law and became a successful attorney.

In 1775, he was elected to the Provincial Congress and became its secretary. From 1776 until 1783, he served as the attorney general of New Jersey, where he was faced with the difficult task of trying to maintain law and order as the war repeatedly swept through the state.

Paterson is best known for his part in framing the U.S. Constitution as a delegate from New Jersey. After the new Constitution was ratified, Paterson became one of New Jersey's first U.S. senators. From 1790 to 1793, he also served as governor after the death of William Livingston. In 1793, President George Washington appointed William Paterson a justice to the U.S. Supreme Court, where he remained until his death in 1806.

With Stevens's steady guidance, the convention went through the Constitution article by article. David Brearley, who was chief justice of the New Jersey Supreme Court, was the person given the task of defending the Constitution. As one of the delegates at

## Preamble to the U.S. Constitution

*We the People of the United States, in Order to form a more perfect Union, establish Justice, insure domestic Tranquility, provide for the common defence, promote the general Welfare, and secure the Blessings of Liberty to ourselves and our Posterity, do ordain and establish this Constitution for the United States of America.*

Chief Justice of the New Jersey Supreme Court, David Brearley represented Philadelphia at the state convention to ratify the U.S. Constitution. He helped persuade the delegates to make New Jersey the third state to ratify the document. *(New Jersey Historical Society)*

Philadelphia, his opinions were very persuasive. After three days of careful consideration and discussion, on December 18, 1787, New Jersey became the third state to ratify the new U.S. Constitution. Delaware was the first state to ratify the constitution, followed by Pennsylvania.

Governor Livingston, whose firm guidance had seen New Jersey through the war and the difficult times that followed, had been extremely concerned about the future of the republic under the Articles of Confederation. When New Hampshire became the ninth state to ratify, and the Constitution was put into effect, Governor Livingston told the legislature, "We are now arrived at the auspicious Era, which, I confess, I have most earnestly wished to see. Thanks to God that I have lived to see it."

# New Jersey Time Line

## 1497
★ John Cabot sails past the Jersey shore.

## 1524
★ Giovanni de Verrazano sails past the Jersey shore.

## 1609
★ Henry Hudson "discovers" the Hudson River and the surrounding area, and claims it for the Dutch. Hudson is the first recorded European to go ashore in New Jersey.

## 1618
★ The Dutch establish a trading post at Bergen.

## 1624
★ The Dutch West Indies Company establish New Amsterdam and builds Fort Nassau on the Delaware River.

## 1629
★ The Dutch establish Pavonia, present-day Jersey City.

## 1638
★ The New Sweden Company settle along the Delaware River; establishing New Sweden.

## 1643

★ Johan Printz becomes the leader of New Sweden.
★ Swedes build Fort Elfsborg near Fort Nassau.

## 1655

★ Peter Stuyvesant, Dutch governor of New Netherland, attacks the Swedes at Fort Elfsborg; the Swedes surrender without a fight.

## by 1660

★ Smallpox and other European diseases decimate the Lenni Lenape population.

## 1664

★ Concession and Agreement of the Lords Proprietors of New Caesaria of New Jersey states that all free persons, including women, who are worth 50 pounds are landholders (does not include slaves and indentured servants).
★ **May:** James, duke of York, brother of English king Charles II and head of the British navy, sends ships to New Netherland.
★ **September 8:** New Amsterdam governor Peter Stuyvesant, outnumbered, surrenders without a fight. The area is renamed New York in James's honor. The duke of York grants the land between the Hudson and Delaware Rivers to Sir George Carteret and John, Lord Berkeley.

## 1667

★ The British colony is divided into East Jersey and West Jersey. It is named Jersey for Sir George Carteret, who was also governor of the Isle of Jersey.

## 1682

★ Elizabeth Carteret, the widow of George Carteret, sells the land of East Jersey to the Quakers.

## 1702

★ The royal charter granted to New Jersey becomes a crown colony under the governor of New York.

## 1738

★ New Jersey becomes self-governing.

## 1746

★ The College of New Jersey (now Princeton) is started by Presbyterians.

## 1763

★ William Franklin, a son of Benjamin Franklin, becomes governor of New Jersey.

## 1774

★ **December 22:** New Jersey's "tea party," which becomes known as the Greenwich Tea Burning, occurs.

## 1776

★ **May 10:** In Philadelphia, the Second Continental Congress convenes.

★ **June 19:** The New Jersey Provincial Congress arrests William Franklin and takes control of the government.

★ **June 21:** The New Jersey Provincial Congress votes 53-3 to sever ties with the British.

★ **July 1:** The Continental Congress approves the Declaration of Independence. General Washington's troops build Fort Lee.

★ **July 2:** The first New Jersey constitution is ratified. It omits the word "male," enabling women to vote until November 16, 1807, when the New Jersey legislature rescinds it.

★ **July 4:** The Continental Congress approves the Declaration of Independence.

★ **November 16:** The British take Fort Washington, and Washington evacuates Fort Lee.

★ **November 20:** Washington retreats from Fort Lee for New Bridge Landing and Steuben House.

★ **November 23–December 3:** Washington's retreat continues. He and his troops travel through Princeton to the Delaware River.

- ★ **December 7–8:** Washington and the American troops cross the Delaware River, and the British and the Hessians reach Princeton and Trenton.
- ★ **December 13:** The British capture General Lee in Basking Ridge.
- ★ **December 25:** George Washington and the Continental army (2,400 troops) cross the Delaware River.
- ★ **December 26:** At 4 A.M., Washington's troops start their march to Trenton. They defeat the Hessian troops at the Old Barracks.

## 1777

- ★ **January 1:** Charles Cornwallis assumes the command of the British army in Princeton.
- ★ **January 2:** The Second Battle of Trenton is fought.
- ★ **January 3:** The Battle of Princeton is waged, and General Washington's troops defeat the British.
- ★ **January 6–May 28:** George Washington and his army winter at Morristown.
- ★ **September 26:** The British take Philadelphia.
- ★ **October 22:** The Americans defeat the Hessian soldiers.
- ★ **November 15:** The British capture Fort Mifflin in Pennsylvania.
- ★ **December–May:** Washington's 12,000 troops winter at Valley Forge, Pennsylvania.

## 1778

- ★ **March 21:** The Hancock House massacre occurs, where the British and Loyalists kill patriots.
- ★ **June 28:** The Battle of Monmouth is fought. "Molly Pitcher" (Mary Ludwig Hays McCauley) brings water to the troops at the Battle of Monmouth. She then takes her husband's place when he is unable to fight.
- ★ **December 11:** Washington has his headquarters in Wallace House. His troops winter in Middlebrook in the Watchung Mountains.

## 1779

- ★ **August 19:** The American major Henry Lee attacks the British fort at Paulus Hook (now Jersey City).
- ★ **October 28:** The British under Major John Simcoe attack the

Americans from Elizabethtown to Bound Brook and at the Somerset Courthouse, Millstone.

★ **December 1:** Washington and his army winter at Morristown. It is thought to be the worst winter in a century.

## 1780

★ **June 7–23:** The Battle of Springfield is fought, as well as a battle in Elizabethtown and the Springfield invasion.

★ **July 1–8:** Washington has his headquarters at Dey Mansion in Wayne.

## 1783

★ **January:** The Articles of Peace are signed.

★ **February:** The British stop fighting.

★ **April:** The remaining Loyalists in New Jersey leave the country for Canada or England.

★ **June 30:** Princeton becomes the temporary capital of the country at Nassau Hall.

★ **August 23:** George and Martha Washington arrive at Rockingham.

★ **September 3:** The British and Americans sign a peace treaty in Paris, France.

## 1787

★ **December 18:** New Jersey becomes the third state.

# New Jersey Historical Sites

## FORT LEE

**Fort Lee Historic Park**   Displays at this park tell the story of Washington's retreat on November 18, 1776, after being defeated at Fort Lee.

>*Address:* Hudson Terrace, Fort Lee, NJ 07024
>*Phone:* 201-461-1776

## HADDONFIELD

**Indian King Tavern**   This is the site where the New Jersey Assembly approved the adoption of the Great Seal of New Jersey and where later the assembly voted to use the word "state" instead of "colony."

>*Address:* 233 Kings Highway, Haddonfield, NJ 08033
>*Phone:* 856-429-6792
>*Web Site:* www.state.nj.us/dep/parksandforests/
>        virtual_tours/indian_king_tavern.html

## MONMOUTH

**Monmouth Battlefield State Park**   This was where the Battle of Monmouth was fought on June 28, 1778, a political victory for Washington. The battle is reenacted every fourth weekend in June.

*Address:* 347 Freehold-Englishtown Road, Manalapan,
   NJ 07726
*Phone:* 732-462-9616
*Web Site:* www.state.nj.us/dep/parksandforests/parks/
   monbat.html

# MORRISTOWN

**Morristown National Historical Park**    This includes sites occupied by Washington and his troops in 1779–80, including the Jacob Ford Mansion, which was used as Washington's military headquarters during the winter of 1779–80.

   *Address:* 30 Washington Place, Morristown, NJ 07960-4299
   *Phone/fax:* 973-539-8361
   *Web Site:* www.nps.gov/morr

# PRINCETON

**Princeton Battlefield State Park**    This was the site of the battle in Princeton on January 3, 1777, where Washington's troops defeated the British.

   *Address:* 500 Mercer Road, Princeton, NJ 08540-4810
   *Phone:* 609-921-0074
   *Web Site:* www.state.nj.us/dep/parksandforests/parks/
      princeton.html

# RIVER EDGE

**Steuben House**    This house was given to Baron Von Steuben for his help during the Revolution.

   *Address:* 1209 Main Street, River Edge, NJ 07661
   *Phone:* 201-487-1739

# RINGWOOD

**Long Pond Ironworks State Park**    The ironworks was started by Peter Hasenclever in 1766.

*Address:* c/o Ringwood State Park, 1304 Sloatsburg Road,
    Ringwood, NJ 07456
*Phone:* 973-962-7031
*Web Site:* www.state.nj.us/dep/parksandforests/parks/
    longpond.html

## STANHOPE

**Waterloo Village**    William Allen and Joseph Turner started the
Andover Iron Works in 1760. Waterloo Village is now a restored
historic site, with a working farm and a traditional Lenni Lenape
village.

*Address:* 525 Waterloo Road, Stanhope, NJ 07874
*Phone:* 973-347-0900
*Web Site:* www.waterloovillage.org/home.html

## TITUSVILLE

**Washington Crossing State Park**    This is where Washington and
his troops landed after crossing the Delaware River on December
25, 1776, before marching on Trenton and defeating the Hessian
troops.

*Address:* 355 Washington Crossing-Pennington Road,
    Titusville, NJ 08560-517
*Phone:* 609-737-0623
*Web Site:* www.state.nj.us/dep/parksandforests/parks/
    washcros.html

# Further Reading

## BOOKS

Fradin, Dennis Brindell. *The New Jersey Colony*. Chicago: Children's Press, 1991.

McCormick, Richard P. *New Jersey from Colony to State*. New Brunswick, N.J.: Rutgers University Press, 1964.

Pomfret, John E. *Colonial New Jersey: A History*. New York: Scribner's, 1973.

Steward, Mark. *New Jersey History*. Chicago: Heineman, 2003.

Streissguth, Thomas. *New Jersey (The Thirteen Colonies)*. San Diego: Lucent, 2001.

Weatherly, Myra. *The New Jersey Colony*. Chanhassen, Minn.: Childs World, 2003.

## WEB SITES

"Electronic New Jersey: A digital archive of New Jersey History." Available online. URL: http://sccol.rutgers.edu/njh/. Downloaded on September 2, 2003.

Green, Howard L. "A Synopsis of New Jersey History." Available online. URL: http://www.state.nj.us/hangout/synopsis.htm. Updated in July 1996.

Monmouth University. "New Jersey History Page." Available online. URL: http://hawkmail.monmouth.edu/~njhist. Downloaded on September 2, 2003.

New Jersey Commerce & Economic Growth Commission. "New Jersey History." Available online. URL: http://www.state.

nh.us/travel/history.shtml. Downloaded on September 2, 2003.

New Jersey Division of Parks and Forestry. "American Revolutionary War Sites." Available online. URL: http://www.state.nj.us/dep/parksandforests/special/revolution. Downloaded on September 3, 2003.

New Jersey Division of Parks and Forestry. "Virtual Tours of NJ State Parks, Forests and Historic Sites." Available online. URL: http://www.state.nj.us/dep/parksandforests/virtual_tours/index.html. Downloaded on September 3, 2003.

"New Jersey History & Culture Web Sites." Available online. URL: http://library.atlantic.edu/amato/NJ%20History%20Links.html. Downloaded on September 2, 2003.

"Roots-L New Jersey: History." Available online. URL: http://www.rootsweb.com/roots-l/usa/nj/history.html. Updated on September 25, 2001.

# Index

Page numbers in *italic* indicate photographs. Page numbers in **boldface** indicate box features. Page numbers followed by m indicate maps. Page numbers followed by c indicate time line entries. Page numbers followed by t indicate a table or graph.

# D

damage, from war 75–76
Dark Ages (Middle Ages) xiii
Dayton, Jonathan 85, 85, 86
Declaration of Independence
    53
        approval of 91c
        Abraham Clark and 82
        first paragraph of **53**
        New Jersey representatives
            at signing 51
        uniting of colonies follow-
            ing 51
deer 6–7
Delaware 11, 84
Delaware Indians. *See* Lenni
    Lenape
Delaware River
        customs duties collected by
            Edmund Andros 37
        and Fort Nassau 4, 89c
        and Lenni Lenape 4
        and New Sweden 18–19,
            89c
        and retreat of Continental
            army 52, 91c
        Washington's crossing of
            56, 56, 92c
De La Warr, Lord 4
desertion 63
devaluation, of currency 77
Dey Mansion 93c
*Discovery* (ship) **3**
disease 10, 90c
division, of New Jersey 29,
    30m, 90c. *See also* East New
    Jersey; West New Jersey
Dominion of New England
    (1687–1689) 38m, 39
Dutch. *See also* New Amsterdam;
    New Netherland
        and Charles (prince of
            Wales) **21**

claims on Hudson River
    89c
colonial claims on New
    Jersey 1–4
colonies and purchases in
    New World xv–xvi
conquest of New Sweden
    19
and Dutch West India
    Company **14**
exploration of New World
    xv–xvi, 16
and Kieft's Indian War 18
land claims 12m
land ownership 9
and New Sweden 19
and Pavonia 89c
recapture of New Jersey
    29
religious tolerance 15
settlers in New Jersey
    11–18
and slave trade **32**
trade competition with
    England 22
trading post at Bergen 89c
Dutch East India Company 2, 3,
    **14**
Dutch settlement (Van Wagoner
    homestead) 15
Dutch West India Company 14,
    **14**
        establishment of New Ams-
            terdam 89c
        forming of 11
        land ownership in New
            Netherland 15

# E

early explorers 1–10
early settlers **24**
east coast of North America xvi,
    22

east coast of North America 22
Eastern Woodland Indians 4. *See
    also specific tribes*
East New Jersey 30m
        Edmund Andros and 37
        Elizabeth Carteret and 29,
            90c
        Sir George Carteret and
            **26,** 29
        Lewis Morris and **43**
        William Penn and **36**
        and postwar New Jersey
            monetary policy 76–77
        proprietors and speculators
            29, 31, 33, 35, 37
        slavery issue **33**
economic crisis, postwar
    76–77, **78**
Elfsborg, Fort. *See* Nya Elfsborg,
    Fort
Elizabethtown (Elizabeth), New
    Jersey
        College of New Jersey **62**
        establishment of 23
        as first capital 27
        William Livingston and **75**
        Simcoe's attack on 93c
        spring 1780 battle 71, 93c
Elizabethtown Associates 24
Elmina (West African fort) 32
England. *See also* British army
        battles with Spain for sea
            supremacy xv
        colonial claims on New
            Jersey 1
        control of colonial trade
            44
        domestic unrest in 17th
            century 20
        domination of east coast of
            North America 19
        and Dutch West India
            Company 14

exploration of New World
xv
William Franklin's exile to
75
and French and Indian War
44
as proprietor of New Jersey
29
royal charters xvi
settlement of New Jersey
23–25
settlers in New Jersey
20–28
severing of ties with 91c
sponsorship of Hudson's
voyages 2, 3, **3**
trade competition with
Netherlands 22
Europe
attitude toward Native
Americans xvii
colonization efforts in 16th
and 17th centuries 1–4
first arrival in New Jersey
89c
and Middle Ages xiii
and Renaissance xiii–xv
explorers, early 1–10

## F

Far East, trade routes to xv
farming and farmers
in colonial New Jersey **34**
and Lenni Lenape 6
postwar depression of
prices 76
role in War for Indepen-
dence 65
Shays's Rebellion 84–85
feathers 8
federal government
and Annapolis Convention
84

and Articles of Confederation **79**
need for revenue sources
82
New Jersey's refusal to
send funds to 81
state representation in
85–86
weakness of, prior to Constitutional Convention
84–85
and western land claims
81
federalism **79,** 81
Fenwick, John 35
financial crisis, postwar 76–77,
**78,** 84–85
First Battle of Trenton 58m
first settlements in New Jersey
11–19
first towns in New Jersey 25m
fishing 6
flogging **33**
Florida, Spanish colonization of
xv
food, as form of currency **7**
food preparation, by Lenni
Lenape 6–7, 9
food shortages 63
Fox, George 31, **31**
France
colonial claims on New
Jersey 1
exploration of New World
xv
and French and Indian War
44
Sir George Carteret and **26**
James II and **21**
Lafayette and **67**
Verrazano's colonial claims
for 1
Franklin, Benjamin 46, 52

Franklin, William
appointment as governor
46–47, 91c
arrest by Patriots 51, 91c
relationship with people of
New Jersey 48
release from prison 75
"freeholders" 74
free trade 79
French, Susanna **75**
French and Indian War (Seven
Years' War) 44, 55
fur trade 11, 18

## G

Gage, Thomas **54**
galleons xv, xvi
game, preparation by Lenni
Lenape 6–7
General Assembly 51
George II (king of Great Britain)
22
Georgia 45, 46
Germantown, Battle of 65
Germany **55**
Glorious Revolution **21**, 39
Gloucester, New Jersey 11
Gosnold, Bartholomew xvi
government, federal. *See* federal
government
government, of New Jersey. *See*
Concession and Agreement;
Constitution (New Jersey)
governors of New Jersey
Lord Cornbury **42**
William Franklin 46–47,
91c
Andrew Hamilton 40
limited powers of 73
William Livingston **75**
Lewis Morris 42–43, **43**
William Paterson **87**
payment of 46

Nassau, Fort (continued)
     establishment of  4, 11,
          13, 89c
     and Fort Nya Elfsborg  19
     and slaves  32
Nassau Hall (Princeton Univer-
     sity)  76, **83,** 83, 93c
national capital. *See* capital,
     national
Native Americans  xvii. *See also*
     Kieft's Indian War; Lenni
     Lenape; *specific tribes*
     and Dutch West India
          Company  11
     and French and Indian War
          44
     William Livingston and  **75**
     William Penn and  **36**
     population  xvii, 4
     revenge killing by  17
     and Wampum  **7**
navy, English
     battle for New Netherland
          23, 90c
     Sir George Carteret and  **26**
     James (duke of York) as
          admiral of  20, **21**
Navy, U.S.  64
the Netherlands. *See* Dutch
New Amsterdam  13, 22
     and battle for New Nether-
          land  23
     establishment of  4, 11, 89c
     and Kieft's Indian War
          17–18
     migration of families from
          17
     slave auctions  **32**
*The new and unknown world, or*
     *description of America and the*
     *Southland* (Arnoldus Mon-
     tanus) (frontispiece)  16
Newark, New Jersey  24, **62**

New Bridge Landing  91c
New England, Dominion of
     (1687–1689)  38m
Newfoundland  xiii
New Hampshire  **24,** 88
New Haven, Connecticut  24
New Jersey
     and Annapolis Convention
          84
     first towns in  25m
     and New Netherland  11
     as state  73–81, 93c
New Jersey Plan  85, 86
"New Jersey Tea Party"  **46, 48**
New Netherland  4, 11–13,
     12m, 15–16, 18
     beginnings of colony  11
     and Dutch West India
          Company  **14**
     English claims on  22
     and patroonship  **17**
     and slaves  **32**
     surrender to England  23,
          90c
     wampum as currency in  **7**
New Netherland (historic map)
     13
New Sweden  18–19, 89c, 90c
New Sweden Company  89c
New World, Spanish power in
     xv
New York
     and Annapolis Convention
          84
     joint governorship with
          New Jersey  42, **43**
     and patroons  **17**
     stalemate in 1779  69
     tariff dispute with New
          Jersey  79
New York City
     Dutch purchase of  xv
     East New Jersey and  37

     first settlement of New
          Amsterdam  4
     and New Amsterdam  11
     slave auctions  **32**
     and surrender of New
          Netherland  23
     tariff dispute with New
          Jersey  79
     as U.S. capitol  **84**
New York colony, Dutch claims
     on  4
New York state
     and defense of British
          colonies  40
     James II's land grants
          24–25
     and New Netherland  11
     and surrender of New
          Netherland  23, 90c
     and western land claims
          81
Nicolls, Richard  22
     battle for New Netherland
          23
     and the Concession and
          Agreement  27
     as governor of New York
          23
     and land grants  39
     and Puritan settlements in
          New Jersey  **24**
     and rent revolt (1672)  28
nonexportation agreement  49
nonimportation agreement  48,
     49
North America. *See* America
North Carolina  1
Northeast culture area  4
Northern Unami-Unalachtigo
     dialect  4, 5m
Northwest Passage  2–4, **3**
"no taxation without represen-
     tation"  45

Nova Scotia
    Hudson's exploration of
        3–4
    Loyalist exile in 74
    Verrazano's exploration of
        1
    Viking exploration of xiii
Nya Elfsborg, Fort 19, 90c

## O

Oklahoma 10
Orange, Fort 11
Ottoman Turks xv
ownership, of land. *See* land
    ownership

## P

Pacific Ocean, Hudson's search
    for passage to 4
paper bills (currency) 77, **78,** 78
Paris, Treaty of 44, 72, 72, 93c
Parliament
    and Stamp Act 45, 46
    and Sugar Act 45
    and Tea Act 47
    and Townshend Duties 46,
        47
passenger pigeon 8
Paterson, William 86, **87**
    as delegate to Constitu-
        tional Convention 85,
        86
    and New Jersey Plan 85
    and ratification of U.S.
        Constitution 86
Patriots
    conflicts with Loyalists in
        1777 64
    departure from Continental
        Army 52
    Hancock House massacre
        92c
    and Loyalists 51

patroons (patroon system) 15,
    17, **17**
Paulus Hook 92c
Pauw, Michael 15, 17
Pavonia (Jersey City)
    establishment of 15, 17, 89c
    and Kieft's Indian War 17
    and slaves **32**
pelts 10
pence (English) 7
Penn, William 36, **36**
    and East New Jersey land
        deal 29–30
    and Quakers **31,** 35, 37
Pennsylvania
    and abolitionism **33**
    and Annapolis Convention
        84
    and Continental army
        retreat 52
    Fort Mifflin 92c
    Molly Pitcher and **71**
    William Penn and **36**
    Quakers and **31**
    tariff dispute 79
    western land claims 81
Pennsylvania State Regiment of
    Artillery **70**
pensions **71,** 75
Pershing, John J. **67**
Perth Amboy, New Jersey
    William Franklin's arrest
        51
    slave auctions **32**
    war damage to 76
Philadelphia
    David Brearley and 88
    capture by Cornwallis 65,
        92c
    Henry Clinton's departure
        from 66
    and Continental Congress
        48, **83,** 91c

military back pay protest
    march 76, **83**
tariff dispute 79
Washington and Hessians
    in 57
West New Jersey and 37
Piscataway, New Jersey 24
place-names in New Jersey,
    Lenni Lenape origins of **10**
political turmoil, in colonial
    New Jersey 37, 39–40,
    42–43
population
    as of 1670 37
    as of 1700 37
    as of 1790 37
    federal representation
        based on 85, 86
    growth, 1670–1790 35t
    Native Americans xvii, 4
    slaves as percentage of
        **33**
Portugal xv
Potomac River **84**
preamble to the U.S. Constitu-
    tion **87**
Presbyterians 35, 91c
Princeton, Battle of 60, 60–63,
    61m, 92c, 95
Princeton, New Jersey
    William Paterson and **87**
    Quaker meetinghouse 34
    as temporary capital of U.S.
        93c
    U.S. Congress in 76
Princeton Battlefield State Park
    95
Princeton University **62,** 62–63.
    *See also* Nassau Hall
Printz, Johan 18, 90c
prisoners, as New Sweden
    colonists 18
privateers 64–65